PRAISE FOR
BECOMING SPIRITUALLY INTELLIGENT

"Dr. Paul M. Burns has written a must-read book for anyone who values and desires authentic character development and spiritual growth. His excellent integration of the concepts of emotional intelligence, attachment theory, trauma-informed faith, and Christian spiritual formation will guide you through a transformative experience of significant healing and growth. Read this book—and learn from one of the best."

— **Kenneth Logan**, psychologist, professor, and
director of integration, George Fox University
Graduate School of Clinical Psychology

"If you're on a journey toward lasting transformation, Paul M. Burns's book is a guiding star. With a Christ-centered compass and insights from modern neuroscience, he skillfully blends God's timeless wisdom, captivating stories, and practical exercises, making spiritual growth enjoyable, accessible, and doable. I highly recommend it!"

— **Kim Avery**, life coach and author of
The Prayer Powered Entrepreneur

"One day you and your children will be glad you took *Becoming Spiritually Intelligent* to heart. Paul M. Burns introduces a tested way to motivate and measure growth based on attachment—the strongest force in the human brain and heart."

—**Dr. Jim Wilder**, author, coach, and neurotheologian

"Dr. Paul M. Burns tenderly describes the source of so much dysfunction in our society and in our selves: insecurity. His remedy? A simple, powerful, and transformational path beyond insecurity and into deep and real relationships with those who matter most: God, others, and self. For anyone who has even a hint of a desire for the abundant life Christ offers, this book is a needed companion for walking the path to becoming your most loving self."

—**Chad Hall**, president of Coach Approach Ministries

BECOMING SPIRITUALLY INTELLIGENT

BECOMING

SPIRITUALLY

INTELL**IGENT**

NINE PATHS
TOWARD YOUR
MOST LOVING SELF

PAUL M. BURNS

Broadleaf Books
Minneapolis

BECOMING SPIRITUALLY INTELLIGENT
Nine Paths toward Your Most Loving Self

Library of Congress Cataloging-in-Publication Data

Names: Burns, Paul M., author.
Title: Becoming spiritually intelligent : nine paths toward your most loving self / Paul M. Burns.
Description: Minneapolis, MN : Broadleaf Books, [2024] | Includes bibliographical references.
Identifiers: LCCN 2023045609 (print) | LCCN 2023045610 (ebook) | ISBN 9781506497211 (paperback) | ISBN 9781506497228 (ebook)
Subjects: LCSH: Spiritual formation. | Psychology, Religious.
Classification: LCC BV4511 .B86 2024 (print) | LCC BV4511 (ebook) | DDC 248—dc23/eng/20231221
LC record available at https://lccn.loc.gov/2023045609
LC ebook record available at https://lccn.loc.gov/2023045610

Interior illustrations: Mandy Peterson
Cover image: Illustration © 2023 Getty Images by Asya_mix. Flower © 2023 shutterstock by Canatic.
Cover design: 1517 Media

Print ISBN: 978-1-5064-9721-1
eBook ISBN: 978-1-5064-9722-8

CONTENTS

CONTENTS

INTRODUCTION

The journey that led to this book is a very personal one. My wife and I had recently adopted our first child. I was pastoring a small but very active church, writing my first book, serving as a denominational leader, and doing too many other things to mention. Meanwhile, we were just figuring out how to survive as parents and not do lasting harm to our child. How could we nurture our child into a loving, secure, compassionate, responsible person?

At the same time, I had begun a doctor of ministry program in which I was studying how human beings can learn to love more like Jesus did. When asked what the most important commandment is, Jesus answered by quoting the Torah, "You shall love the Lord your God with all your heart, and with all your soul, and with all your mind, and with all your strength" (Deut 6:5). The second is this: "'You shall love your neighbor as yourself.' There is no other commandment greater than these" (Mark 12:30–31). I was worried that the church was failing—miserably—in this regard, and I wanted to study what was preventing Christians from loving well.

It's not that the church was failing to *preach* about loving God and loving neighbors as themselves; I'd heard—and preached—countless such sermons. It's that all that preaching wasn't resulting in more loving people. Or maybe it was but only in exceptional cases. The love of God that I see in the life of Christ was not flowing out of the people bearing his name. I suspected that the problem had more to do with humans and less to do with the divine.

As I began to look at the research, I discovered my suspicion was far more correct than I thought. In my doctoral program, I became interested in human development, human behavior, and brain function, and I began to research answers to the questions that occupied my attention. What is the source of the blockage that keeps God's love from flowing? And how can we remove those blocks? I developed a model and an assessment called the GPS (God-Personal-Social) Spiritual Inventory, which serves as the basis for this book. It is intended to measure the level of what we could call "lovingness" we share with God, self, and neighbor. It helps identify the blockages that disrupt our ability to receive and share love.

In the midst of all these responsibilities, I also began experiencing panic attacks and paralyzing anxiety. Everything seemed to be jeopardized. I had to face my own mental crisis and learn to live with it—while somehow managing all my commitments, including parenting and preaching and going to school. That's when my study became a matter of survival.

The first Sunday after my first major bout with anxiety, I sat in my study before the church service, paralyzed with fear. Later I would learn the signs of a panic attack; at that point, however, all I knew is that I felt immobilized. How could I lead worship and preach? How could I even manage to greet people as they entered the sanctuary? Everything felt impossible.

If I had had to act lovingly toward another person in that moment—by listening to their pain or helping them in some way—I feel certain I could not have done so. My own fear was too great.

I'll tell you in a bit what ended up happening that morning. In that moment, all I knew is that I felt too insecure, too fearful, and too anxious to offer anything approximating love to anyone else.

This book is the product of my research and my experience. It represents my current understanding of my ever-evolving understanding of human development in relationship with God, ourselves, and others. It brings together my practice of pastoring, coaching, and counseling others on spiritual intelligence. I hope it helps you get in touch with your most secure and loving self.

CAN WE BECOME MORE LOVING?

As I began my dissertation research, I was looking for an assessment of how Christians were doing at loving like Jesus. I came across an enormous six-year study done by Barna Research, *Maximum Faith: Live like Jesus*. George Barna identified ten stops on the way to becoming a mature follower of Christ. Through surveying self-professed Christians in the United States, he showed the percentage of people who had reached the various stages of development.

About 90 percent of those surveyed were stuck on the fourth stop: confessing sins and asking Christ to be their savior. The final six stops, in this frame, are stops of transformation. Only .5 percent of the people surveyed said they had entered the final two phases: enjoying a profound intimacy with and love for God and experiencing a profound compassion and love for humanity.

Barna concluded that 90 percent of Christians in America live indistinguishably from those in the surrounding culture. Their faith and practice had not resulted in a deep love of God and neighbor. So I devoted my efforts to understanding why. What is keeping us from experiencing God's love and being a conduit of it?

In my ministry, I have witnessed wonderful moments of love that reminded me of the Jesus of the New Testament and the Jesus I experienced in my heart. I have also witnessed selfishness, pettiness, meanness, and downright hatred—in some cases, from the very same people with whom I witnessed amazing love. And as I observe the person that I spend the most time with—myself—I see all the same things. I see myself loving all kinds of people . . . and then the next moment yelling at the people I love the most, like my children or my wife.

So how can we become more loving? Is it possible to grow into lovingness? These questions assume that we are basically not loving enough. They might sound premised on the notion that through practice or learning, we can make ourselves more loving and less hateful, unforgiving, and selfish.

But I have come to believe that we can't. You can't just *make* yourself more loving—at least not when you are feeling insecure. Insecurity and love don't go together. A quick note: If that worries you because you feel insecure a lot of the time, just hold on.

We all have an insecure self. You are not alone, and there's hope for all of us.

Let's look at how love and insecurity are incompatible. Our species developed, like all others, to survive. To survive individually, we need safety and nourishment. To survive as a species, we need sex to reproduce—which, you may be disappointed or relieved to hear, we won't be dealing with in this book. But these survival instincts go deep in our DNA and culture. Some would argue that even love is a survival instinct, and they would be right—*if* their definition of love, that is, is a transactional one. If love means pleasing other people so they will protect you or nourish you in some way, then yes: love is a survival instinct.

But is that true love? Is that the love we see in a mother who protects her young at all costs—including, if necessary, the loss of her own life? Is that the love we see exemplified in the life of Christ? Is that the love we see when we hear about people like Mother Teresa and Father Damien, who gave up everything to take care of people with leprosy? Or even the love we sometimes see in young children, who forgive another kid for pushing them even when the other child refuses to apologize?

This kind of love—self-sacrificial, self-giving love that is promised nothing in return—runs directly against our evolutionary survival instincts. And we can't love in this way unless we have a sense of security. The secure self does not have to spend all its energy on protecting and feeding oneself. The secure self is free to give and even sacrifice—to care for others for their own sake and not for any other reason.

What I am calling the *secure self* is the person that God created you to be rather than what the world has raised you to be. Your secure self can love like Christ loved without even a thought. Love can become natural. When we start taking seriously the idea of the secure self, our main question will move from how we can become more loving to how we can become more secure *so that* we can love like Christ.

I need to acknowledge that I am coming from a perspective that you might not share. As a Christian, I believe there is no permanent security in the world in which we live. Yes, we might feel secure when our significant others or caregivers show themselves as dependable, when we have money to pay the bills, when we have a vocation that gives us purpose, and when we hold the respect of our peers. We might feel secure when our health is good, when we have a safe place to sleep, when our nation is at peace, when we don't hear of mass shootings every week, when there are no earthquakes or hurricanes, when loved ones aren't dying, when our significant other isn't breaking up with us, when we are at the body weight that suits us, and when we are not facing our own death.

But we never have all that, do we? When, then, are we secure? If love requires security, how can we love in an insecure world?

If you find your sense of security in these things, you will spend all your energy trying to stop the thing that none of us can stop: dying. And in doing so, you will have nothing left to give that we call love. You will not be a loving person; you will just be a surviving person. You will cast about for something that looks and feels like love. What if the secure self doesn't depend on any of these external factors?

Becoming Spiritually Intelligent will focus on how to cultivate a secure attachment to God—an attachment that will become the foundation of security you will need to love others in the way of Christ. To attach to God, you will need to learn to self-differentiate, whether it be from your family of origin, your work, your political party, or even your faith tradition. By attaching your life to God and self-differentiating from those around you, you will find yourself freed *for* empathy and *from* the need to please or control others. So we'll talk about self-differentiation—the capacity to distinguish your own feelings and thoughts from those of others—and about empathy too. In that way, you will be truly spiritually intelligent—able to love God, love yourself, and love and care for others for their own sake and not your own.

WHAT IS SPIRITUAL INTELLIGENCE?

There is no one definition of spiritual intelligence. Spiritual intelligence traces its history from the theory of multiple intelligences introduced by Howard Gardner; that, in turn, inspired Daniel Goleman, Peter Salovey, John Mayer, and others to develop the theory of emotional intelligence. The main thrust of these theories is that IQ is not the only factor in determining success in life. In fact, emotional intelligence has proven to be a much greater predictor of educational and vocational success. Emotional intelligence comprises awareness and management of one's emotional life, along with the capacity to understand the emotions of others and relate empathetically to them.

Some theorists view spiritual intelligence as its own separate intelligence. Some versions of it involve the ability to connect with the transcendent reality of the universe, which may or may not involve connection with a divine being. Others define it simply as the ability to integrate other intelligences in order to think beyond the known world.

My version of spiritual intelligence builds on the basic theory of emotional intelligence. Emotional intelligence focuses on our relationships with ourselves and others, but it does not explicitly account for a relationship with God. So my theory of spiritual intelligence involves healthy, loving relationships with self, others, *and* God. I define spiritual intelligence as the ability to receive God's love and to love oneself and others in the same way.

There are correlations among our emotional health, our level of empathy for others, and the depth of our relationship with a personal, loving, forgiving God. Many Christian leaders have preached about relationship with God but have ignored emotional health and empathy. They have taught that all you need is belief in Christ, and you will go to heaven. Great news, sure. But what about your life *now*? On the other hand, if you've seen a therapist or read books about mental health and relationships, you may be very familiar with the concepts of self-differentiation and empathy. But you may not have connected those to your image of or relationship with God.

While there's no one definition of spiritual intelligence, I believe there's one singular model of it: Jesus. You don't have to be a Christian to believe that Jesus of Nazareth was the most spiritually intelligent person to have ever lived. One way to write this book would be to look at the life of Christ to learn what spiritual intelligence looks like in action. That's not how I've chosen to write it. Instead, I will share the research I've done in attachment theory, spiritual formation, and brain science. 1 will describe a model of Christ-centered spiritual intelligence, and in the epilogue, I'll describe a spiritual intelligence inventory, which is a statistically valid psychometric assessment of spiritual health, that I created. Throughout the book, I'll tell some stories from my own life and from the conversations I've had with people I've coached and counseled over the years. And while this isn't a study of Jesus, we will look at stories from Scripture, including some from the life of Jesus, that illuminate aspects of spiritual intelligence.

My research shows there are three major facets of spiritual intelligence: depth of attachment to God, level of self-differentiation, and capacity for empathy. Each facet of spiritual intelligence has three "paths" within it. You could think of these nine paths as ways that a particular facet of spiritual intelligence manifests.

This book will take you through the nine paths toward spiritual intelligence. In essence, there are nine practices that comprise spiritual intelligence. Each chapter includes, at the end, reflection questions, spiritual intelligence exercises, and a guided prayer.

Before we begin our journey, I want to introduce you to the foundational concepts of this model of spiritual intelligence.

A BIT OF BRAIN SCIENCE

Our brains allow us to critically examine the world around us and within us. They house our ability to connect with others. They facilitate imagination and creativity.

The brain does not work very well, however, when it senses a threat, whether real or imagined. All the higher functions of our brain, which separate us from the rest of the animals on the planet, shut down when our fear centers run on hyperdrive.

In a state of fear or anger, we revert to our ancient evolutionary roots. Our brain prepares our bodies to fight like a bear, for flight like a bird, or to freeze like a possum. Thank God we have these instincts; they are meant to keep us alive. If our brains are left in their default, survival-focused mode, however, we will become self-centered, controlled by our emotions, unable to trust others, and incapable of empathy.

Therefore, if we are to talk about how a person loves like Christ, it will be helpful to understand how our brains can inhibit or facilitate it.

Security is truly a state of mind. If you believe you are safe, then your brain will act accordingly. The problem is that anything perceived as a threat triggers your fear center before it reaches your critical thinking center. When your fear center is activated, it hampers your ability to see and think clearly.

Many things can make us afraid, and we can even live under a constant state of threat. The COVID-19 pandemic put many of us in a near-constant state of insecurity. Our higher brain powers as a society were reduced. We were more reactive to everything and everyone. We were more likely to argue and retreat to find safety. Our survival instincts kicked into high gear. Overall, it wasn't a great season for loving others.

Another important feature of the brain is called neuroplasticity. Up until the last few decades, it was widely thought that once you reached the age of twenty-five or so, your brain hardened like dry cement. We assumed it could not really change, adapt, or heal. Now we understand that the brain is incredibly adaptable—more like plastic than cement. When you begin doing things differently, your brain can literally be reshaped. If you have a stroke, the part of the brain that controls the left side of your body may be damaged, but you can learn to reuse your left side through other networks of neurons in your brain. You can even grow new neurons.

Think of neural networks like a series of pathways. The more you walk down a pathway, the easier it gets. These pathways form through habit. The more regularly you do something, the easier it gets. Forming new pathways and abandoning old ones will take time and effort, but it is possible. Consider trust as a neural network, a pathway in your brain. If the trust road was never established in your brain as a baby and nurtured as a child, then it will be very hard for you to trust others—no less an invisible God. Trusting others will feel like walking into an untouched jungle—scary and confusing.

Perhaps you were raised by trustworthy caregivers, but your trust got broken through a betrayal from a close friend or romantic partner. It's like trees that fell on your path or a rockslide that buried it up. It makes it hard to go down that way again. The field of neuropsychology has shown that broken trust is almost like a stroke: it damages the parts of our brain that facilitate trust. Neuroplasticity tells us that the brain can heal around the damage. Brain damage that is caused in relationships can be healed through new relationships. When we are heard, felt, and seen in our pain or shame—when another person approaches us with compassion and without judgment—we can learn to trust again. If we can learn to trust, then we are on our way to being able to love.

No, facing the things that make you insecure does not take brain surgery! But it is indeed a "treatment" of the brain. When your brain is led by the parts that facilitate wisdom and loving connection with others, you can live in the image of God imprinted on all people. If not, you will think and act more like the rest of the animal kingdom. Finding ways of gaining a sense of security is key.

HOW HEALTHY ATTACHMENTS SHAPE AND RESHAPE YOUR SENSE OF SECURITY

Long before you knew anything about God, even before you could speak or crawl, a belief system was forming in you. These beliefs would go on to shape the way you behave in all your relationships, including how you relate or don't relate to God. They are beliefs about yourself and about others. Do I matter? If I cry out, will I be heard? Can I expect to be loved no matter what? Is the world a scary place to hide from or a place of endless wonder to be explored?

According to attachment theorists, this foundation deep within your psyche explains why you act the way you do, why you feel the way you do, and why you believe what you believe. The ways you behave, feel, and believe derive from the answers to two questions: Am I worthy of being loved? Can I trust others to love me?

The answers to these questions began to form from the moment you entered the world. Did your caregivers come when you cried? Did they feed you when you were hungry? What was the expression on their faces when they found you in distress? Did they show concern, distaste, anger, or nothing at all? Did your caregivers have well-managed emotional health, or did their anxiety or depression shut them down? All these things and more impact the answers to these two questions.

In the best scenario—when your caregivers were well cared for themselves and were able to respond to you consistently, lovingly, and in a timely manner—you began to believe that your life mattered, that you were worthy of love. Trust was being built. Little by little, the emotional equipment you were born with was being hooked up and taught to operate. A sense of self as loved and a sense that others can be trusted began to form. A capacity for loving your caregivers slowly formed. You began to seek out your caregivers with your eyes. Your little hands began to reach back to grasp the loving hands that held you. Their smiles made you smile and vice versa. If you were upset, their presence comforted you. And when your distress abated, you were able to happily play and explore your environment. The path for intellectual, emotional, and spiritual development was being paved within your brain and your soul. Security was being formed. It was complete when you began to return love to your parents.

I will never forget the first time my son returned my love. When I traveled for work, I would always miss him and be glad to see him when I returned. But until he was around nine months old, there was little evidence that he knew I was gone. After a particularly long trip, I entered the house. He saw me, his face lit up, and he began crawling toward me yelling, "Dadadadada-dadadadada!" I scooped him up, and he clung to me with all the strength he had in his little arms. It's hard to convey the joy of that moment.

What I am describing is referred to as a secure attachment. That's the best scenario for starting life. It makes loving others, trusting others, and receiving love from others relatively easy because you were bathed in love and trust from the beginning. Attachment theory pioneer John Bowlby described a person with secure attachment as having three qualities:

1. A sense of self-worth

2. A belief in the helpfulness of others

3. A favorable model on which to build future relationships

The ability to receive love from others and express love to others in relationship is essential. Having a secure attachment is essential, too, for a vibrant and healthy spiritual life.

None of us was raised by perfect parents, however. Even the healthiest and most loving parents have their bad days fueled by lack of sleep, the stress of hearing a baby cry all the time, outside stressors, and bouts of anxiety or depression. All these things, among others, can create ambivalence about the answers to our two questions.

Implicit thoughts entered our little baby minds: Am I really loved? Or am I only loved when I don't cry? Should I hide my feelings if it makes Mom mad? Or do I have to cry louder and longer to get what I need? Or is there no point in crying because nobody answers anyway? All these little baby ruminations begin to set a pattern that, if left unattended, will set the pattern for our future relationships.

Our ability to feel secure in ourselves and with others comes from our caregivers. This security—or lack of it—will shape who we become and how we relate to others. If secure, then we will be able to love people just for who they are and not for what we can get from them. If secure, then we can trust other people to love us without having to hide who we are.

If insecure, we will spend our energy trying to please or manipulate people so they will love us because we don't trust that we are truly worthy of being loved. Or, on the other end of the insecurity spectrum, we will try to keep people at a distance or control them because we can't trust that they are capable of being loving people. Love seems either hard to get or hard to believe in.

From a neuroscience perspective, we could say this about insecure attachment: the pathway of self-worth and the pathway of trusting others may not have been well established. Meanwhile, the pathways of pleasing, avoiding, or controlling others have been well established and perhaps even paved. That's where the plastic, malleable quality of our brains is needed. New pathways of self-worth and trust can be forged. The method of creating a more secure self happens the same way the old, more insecure self was formed: through our relationships with those we rely on.

HOW ATTACHMENT TO GOD CAN LEAD TO A SECURE SELF

Jesus told the teacher Nicodemus that he must be "born again" (John 3:3). We were born and raised in this earthly realm; we must be born in the heavenly realm. Many people have suggested that this passage is all about salvation. And it is, in a way. But it's also about psychology, and attachment, and discipleship. If born again, we must be raised again. Being raised again is what the church might call *discipleship*: following Jesus. Instead of following around Mom and Dad as we did as children, we follow Jesus. We learn our value and values from Christ. We learn to trust from Christ. We need to be reparented. For many people, this reparenting happens from new people in their lives.

Taking God out of this, you can see this principle at work by watching kids as new people become important to them. Imagine that one day your kid comes home and says he wants a different haircut. Rather than the nice, neat short haircut you instructed the barber to give him, he wants to grow out his hair on the top and shave it all around the side—an undercut. Where did he get that idea? He wants to be more like someone else, someone at school he admires perhaps or a celebrity. Why? The realm of kid-dom requires a different set of survival skills than living at home with his parents does. Eight hours a day, he is surrounded by a new group of people. To be accepted, he will have to adapt to them. We conform to the people we rely on for our survival.

For better or worse, we are shaped by the people and environment that raised us. We can be reshaped by God and God's people through new relationships that show us our worth and show themselves to be trustworthy. A secure attachment with God will result in becoming more like the person that God created you to be than the person the world raised you to be. We'll look at attachment with God in part I of the book.

HOW SELF-DIFFERENTIATION CAN FREE YOUR GOD-GIVEN SELF

Self-differentiation, which we'll examine in the chapters of part II, is the ability to distinguish yourself—your thoughts, feelings, and decision-making—from the people around you. The concept comes out of family systems theory, which is the study of how family dynamics shape us and inform how we act. The family that gave us birth has imprinted its values on us and assigned us a role that we are to play. These values and roles have come from generations of the families that we come out of. Without knowing it, we are being shaped by family members long since past. Someone in each generation of your family has played the role that you play now. Our families have been shaped by other systems such as culture, religion, politics, and even sports.

Consider how alcoholism impacts families. Children of alcoholism are much more likely to have codependent tendencies. Codependency causes one to overly rely emotionally on another person. It results in a fear of abandonment. Often a codependent person will rely emotionally on their own children, which spreads the codependency to them.

Codependency is essentially the opposite of self-differentiation. Self-differentiation allows you to consciously choose your own values, have your own opinions, think your own thoughts, and feel your own emotions apart from the ways of your family or church or culture and still maintain a loving engagement.

HOW EMPATHY BECOMES A PATHWAY FOR GOD'S LOVE

The study of empathy has exploded in the last several years. Most researchers view empathy as a good force, one the world greatly needs. A few theorists suggest empathy drains our ability to care, and that it's an unhelpful way to pass around the anxiety of our society. Both are correct. Healthy empathy—the capacity to understand and share the feelings of another person who is not fulfilling some emotional need of our own—is wonderful and needed. Think about a time someone showed that they recognized what you were going through. It feels like being bathed in sunlight. Receiving empathy means being heard, felt, and understood by another. It is what we all desperately want and need.

Unhealthy empathy is not really empathy at all. Empathy that is held captive by a need to please or control is purely self-centered, a survival instinct. It is an attempt to get what you need or want from others. In my experience, people with a low level of self-differentiation and high empathy are starved of emotional support. They are trying to get what they need from everyone they come across, and they use empathy to get it. They never even know they are doing it.

When we have a healthy attachment with God, which enables us to self-differentiate from the world around us, we will be free to love other people for their sake, not ours. Empathy—which we'll look at in part III—becomes a pathway for God's love to pour into the world through us.

BEFORE YOU BEGIN YOUR JOURNEY

So back to that Sunday morning when I was filled with so much anxiety and panic right before I had to lead a worship service and preach. As I sat in my office before the service, a song popped into my head, and I found it online. The singer sang of God's presence and power: "The Lord thy God is in the midst of thee." I must have listened to it seven times. When it was time for the worship service to start, I heard a gentle voice from within say, "Paul, get up, leave your study, and go and engage with the people. By the end of the first hymn, you will be fine."

I timidly walked to the entryway of the sanctuary and began sticking out my hand to greet people, with as much of a smile as I could muster. My hands felt ice cold with fear. Familiar faces smiled warmly at me as I just nodded. I walked to the front and stumbled through some words of welcome.

The sounds of the organ began to pipe, and we began to sing. This next part might sound unbelievable. But by the end of the final verse, the fear had left me. The warmth came back into my hands. My thoughts cleared. As I preached, I knew that I was not alone. God was within me and all around me, in the loving congregation that surrounded me. I was safe and sound again. I was secure, and I could function. Somehow, I sensed in some deep and inexplicable way that all was well.

To be clear, that was not the end of my anxiety. Not by a long shot! I would see my doctor and take medication. I would see a counselor, who would help me unpack my life. I would learn to rest and spend time with myself and God. And then I would dedicate the next several years to understanding what had happened to me—and what was happening to the church—from a spiritual, emotional, and physical perspective. But that morning, I felt the extremes—insecurity and security, terror and safety, fear and love—in a way that I have not forgotten.

Maybe you've had a similar experience. Maybe you've wondered whether you'd ever be able to live differently. Remember when we were talking about neural pathways and how we said that the more you create a pathway, the easier it gets? Neural pathways form through habit. As we learn to live in more spiritually intelligent ways, we form and follow new pathways too.

The nine paths that you will be learning to forge—in your brain and your heart and your relationships—are not linear. As I work with people in coaching and counseling settings, I often ask them which of the nine paths they would like to start with rather than going in some preordained order. I invite you to do the same. As you look at the table of contents, consider which of these nine paths seems most urgent or welcoming to you. Start there!

Last, I invite you to a short self-evaluation exercise as you begin your journey. It will help you to see where your struggle to love is located and point you toward where to focus on your journey. Finish this sentence with as many words or phrases as come to mind:

I can love others except when I _____.

You might want to make a list on a piece of paper or your phone. Keep track of your list so that you can revisit it later in the book. The words on this list will provide clues to the things that are disrupting your ability to live into your most loving self.

Part I

SECURE ATTACHMENT: BEING NURTURED BY GOD

1 | THE PATH OF TRUSTING GOD

What would it take to imagine God as loving and protective and good?

I have coached and pastored a lot of people over the years, and I know that not everyone perceives God—or perhaps any parental figure—as loving. Perhaps you grew up with an image of God as punishing and judging. Perhaps something very painful happened to you, and you felt God should have saved you. Or maybe you've wondered why a good and loving God would allow suffering to the point that you can no longer believe in God. Maybe when you think of church, religion, or the idea of God, it brings up fear and shame or even disgust. Even picking up this book may trigger anxiety in you.

Take a deep breath or two and try something for a moment: Imagine there is no Bible, no religion, no church. Imagine it's just you and some Being who gave you birth into this world. What would this Being be like? Can you see a loving face smiling at you? Is this Being feminine or masculine or some combination of both? Is this Being a light? A loving embrace? A feeling of unconditional love? Write a description of the God you *wish* existed. You might want to paint a picture or just hold that feeling in your mind's eye.

What would a safe God be like for you? What would that Being look like and feel like? Try to imagine that God as you read this book.

WHAT IS TRUST?

Trust happens when we feel safe with a person. This sense of safety that leads to confidence we might call *being secure*.

To lack a sense of safety leads to insecurity. A person who is insecure struggles to trust, and without trust, we lack confidence. When we lack confidence, we struggle to love and be loved, which is at the heart of spiritual intelligence.

Forming a secure attachment with God begins with learning to trust. The psalmist sings, "He who dwells in the shelter of the Most High: who abides under the shadow of the Almighty, He will say to the Lord 'You are my refuge and my stronghold: my God in whom I trust'" (Ps 91:1–2). The Hebrew word *betach* is usually translated as "trust." It most literally means "to seek refuge in." Later in the psalm, the writer compares God to a mother eagle who covers her young under her wings to keep them safe. *Betach* commonly means to trust, to depend on, to feel safe, or to be confident.

Our ability to feel secure begins with the people who took care of us when we were babies. They took us under their wings. They protected us. They fed us. If you had this level of security consistently as a little one, then you were able to have the confidence to grow and learn and have healthy relationships with others. Attachment theorists call this *secure attachment*. It feels safe to *betach* ourselves to loving and protective people.

Attachment theory connects the way we behave in all our human relationships to our earliest attachment-figure relationship, which was typically with our mother. Attachment theory was developed primarily to understand why we act the way we do in times of threat, grief, and loss. An attachment figure is a person you seek to be close to in order to feel safe and secure, just as a baby usually feels safe and secure with their mother. Attaching is a basic survival instinct.

Think for a moment about what you do when you face threat, grief, or loss. Do you seek to be close to someone? Do you want to be alone? Pray? Reach for a bottle? Pour yourself into your work? These are all attachment patterns that began when you were very young. The goal of all these actions is to find comfort and a sense of security. The things or people you seek out in times of crisis are what you trust when your world gets shaky. Being near them gives you a sense of security. If it is a healthy attachment figure, it gives you confidence to face the crisis.

Attachment theory tells us that in a secure attachment, you get two basic things when you connect with your primary attachment figure. The first is a sense of safety. Think of a toddler who goes running to their mommy when they hear a loud and unfamiliar noise. They cling to their mother and ask to be picked up. Their mother comforts them, and they feel safe. Then they are ready to go play again.

That courage to go play is the second thing you receive when you have a secure attachment with your caregiver. It is called a *secure base*. Think of home base in the game of tag. If home base is near, you can run around freely and focus on having fun. If the one who is "it" gets too close, you can simply dash back to home base. Your primary attachment figure provides a secure base for you to run off and courageously explore the world and make friends. Secure attachment forms when your caregiver is nearby, accessible, and attentive.

Eventually, security becomes internalized, and you take it with you wherever you go. You don't need to have a parent nearby to feel secure. But the urge to cling to attachments remains with you even in adulthood.

I lived and worked in New York City on the dreadful day of 9/11. I was far away from my parents, and my wife was in Washington, DC. All the phone lines were jammed, and the sense of terror was palpable. A coworker of mine who lived on Long Island was stuck in the city. So, together, the two of us walked uptown fifty blocks, eventually making it safely to my apartment. To this day, I have a bond with him that will never be broken. We needed each other.

Over the weeks and months to come, it was reported that record numbers of singles were going to bars to connect with people. There was even a 9/11 baby boom. People were clinging to each other; they were parenting each other.

People also began flocking to churches to connect with others and to seek God. My wife and I had been attending a church in New York City, and we suddenly felt a deep need to commit, for the long haul, to something bigger than ourselves. We attended the four-week new members class along with about sixty other people.

During that class, the pastor told us a story about 9/11. The church leaders had decided to open the doors of the sanctuary, which is located on 55th Street and 5th Avenue in Midtown, near the south end of Central Park. They held prayer services all day long. The pastor, in full clergy garb, stood out on 5th Avenue that day and waved frightened and disoriented people into the sanctuary.

One man walked up to the pastor. His white button-down shirt was splattered with the blood of a person who had jumped from one of the towers and landed two feet in front of him. The pastor brought him in, and he collapsed on a pew.

The service was simple, short, and spare. It was mostly Scripture and song and prayer. Traumatized people mostly just need a place to sit and weep or be silent, and the service was meant to be a container for all of that emotion, not a distraction from it. During the service, the pastor read from Psalm 43: God is our refuge and strength, a very present help in times of trouble.

After the service, the man sought out the pastor and asked him, with wonder and urgency in his voice, "What was that poem you read? I have never heard anything like it, and it gave me a great sense of peace. Was it Shakespeare? Tennyson?"

Hearing that psalm on 9/11 didn't change that man's circumstances. Learning that it was from the Bible likely didn't change his life. The terrifying things of the day had still happened. But he had found a refuge for that moment. Trusting God—seeking refuge in God, leaning on God, clinging to God when life gets terrifying—gives you a sense of safety. It gives you a secure base to courageously face whatever threatens you.

It doesn't matter where you are. Believing that God is nearby, accessible, and attentive to your needs can give you security at any time, any place, and in any circumstance.

LEARNING TO TRUST IN GOD

In the Hebrew Scriptures, what Christians call the Old Testament, there is a short book about a woman named Ruth, whose great-grandson would become the most famous king of Israel. The story begins with her husband and his brother both dying. Her mother-in-law has also lost her husband.

Ruth makes the radical choice to follow her deceased husband's mother back to her hometown rather than stay in her own country with her own kin. We don't know what led her to this decision, but I suspect a few things happened. She must have felt truly welcomed into the family by her mother-in-law. Naomi must have been a source of faith and comfort to her. Perhaps Ruth never felt that kind of love and acceptance from her own mother. Perhaps she missed her husband so much that the only way she could feel close to him was to be with the woman who gave him life and raised him. However, it turned out that Naomi had become a source of love and acceptance; she had become a secure base for Ruth. The writer tells us that while her other daughter-in-law kissed her goodbye, "Ruth clung to her."

The Hebrew word for cling is *dabaq*. In modern Hebrew, *dabaq* means "to adhere like glue." Ruth glued herself to Naomi. This is the same word used in Genesis 2:24: "Therefore a man leaves his father and his mother and clings to his wife." To attach is to glue yourself to another person. Ruth then makes a powerful vow to Naomi: "Where you go, I will go; where you lodge, I will lodge; your people shall be my people, and your God my God. Where you die, I will die—there will I be buried. May the Lord do thus and so to me, and more as well, if even death parts me from you!" (Ruth 1:16–17).

However, we should be careful about who we attach ourselves to. What if Naomi hadn't been a reliable or compassionate person? What if she had decided to take advantage of Ruth's vulnerability in some way? When you attach your life to another, you choose to be with them wherever they go. You choose to share their values and be shaped by them.

Think for a moment of baby ducklings when they come out of their eggs. They immediately begin to follow their mother. Attachment is essentially the instinct to stay close. It is a survival instinct. Mama Duck is the source of protection and nourishment. However, human babies are not born ready to follow their caretakers; they rely fully on them for care and safety. Human babies are the most helpless of baby creatures; their survival is totally dependent on their caretakers.

But even the best parents fall short of consistent, loving care. As babies, even with great parenting and care, we are left wondering, to some degree, if we are heard and loved when no one responds to our cries. Perhaps you were met with frustrated, tired faces and voices, and you questioned whether you were loved. Can you trust that others will take care of you? Do you know that you are loved? These doubts cause insecurity, which keeps us from becoming our most loving selves.

Let's shift to the metaphor of a shepherd and sheep. The shepherd is not the mother who gave them birth, but the shepherd becomes an attachment figure. The sheep will follow the shepherd when they learn to trust that if they follow the shepherd, they will be safe and led to food. King David, the great-grandson of Ruth, expressed his relationship with God in terms of a shepherd and sheep in Psalm 23: "The Lord is my shepherd, I shall not want. He makes me lie down in green pastures; he leads me beside still waters; he restores my soul." When you make God your primary attachment figure, you become glued to God. God becomes your caregiver. As you experience God's provision and safekeeping, you grow in your trust. You follow, believing you will be safe and fed.

Dabaq is also used in relationship to God and God's people. Moses urged the Israelites, "If you will diligently observe this entire commandment that I am commanding you, loving the Lord your God, walking in all his ways, and holding fast to him, then the Lord will drive out all these nations before you, and you will dispossess nations larger and mightier than yourselves" (Deut 11:22). When you view God as nearby, accessible, and attentive, you may feel a sense of security even as you face great danger.

So how do you learn to trust God? Think again about Ruth. Ruth had gone through a significant ordeal, and Naomi had loved her through it. I once asked a Sunday school class, "What has drawn you closer to God?" A woman spoke up: "When my husband died, God was all I had. He was there for me. Other people were as well, but God was there in the night when everyone else was gone. Now I can't live without him." Trust comes with experience. It is not something that you just get; you must trust to grow in trust. Trust asks you to take a risk. When you trust God, you make yourself vulnerable to God. God may take you to places that you would not choose to go. You follow, not knowing what will happen, trusting that you will be safe with God. Even as things appear dangerous, you feel safer with God than without God.

We rely on many different sources of security to survive in this life. Trusting God means you rely on God above all other sources. Even when you "walk through the valley of the shadow of death," in King David's words, trusting God means you will fear no evil because God is near. Trusting God does not exempt us from the realities of death and evil. But believing that God will carry us like a shepherd carries a lamb makes all the difference in the way we approach life.

Trust often begins when someone has saved you in some way. Jo-Rommel lived with my family for a year when I was in elementary school through a foreign exchange student program. Once, on a camping trip, I was trying to walk across a stream over a rudimentary rock dam. To my left was a pool, and to my right was a drop-off that led into swift rapids. Jo was in front of me by a few yards when I slipped. I clung to a rock with all my might, and suddenly Jo took my hand and pulled me back up. Later he said, laughing, "Your eyes were as big as moons!" Jo saved me, and my love for and trust in Jo grew as big as moons.

God has saved me more times than I will ever know. Recognizing the ways God has led you through threats, griefs, and losses will nurture your trust. The question you are always asking before you trust someone is "Can I count on this person to be available and responsive when needed?" To trust God, you must give God a chance. Reaching out to God in times of uncertainty and having God respond with love will forge a path of trust in your brain.

BRAIN TRUST

To trust anyone, no less an invisible God, you must believe they care about you just as you are. Their care will activate the parts of your brain needed for trust to emerge. The relational part of your brain is housed in the front right side. It is the part of your brain that allows you to relate to others.

In a state of insecurity, the front parts of your brain don't function well. This is because in crises, the middle and back parts of your brain, which focus on survival, take over. Insecurity keeps you from being able to trust others. You must first feel that you are safe with a person for your fear centers to relax. Only then can you begin to trust them. The love comes over time as you feel that they are safe and care about you.

Trust builds as you feel heard, seen, felt, and understood by another. When you are able to speak about your fears, hurts, and shame to another person and experience nonjudgmental compassion from them, your trust grows.

If you experienced this compassionate love as a baby, then a brain path of trust is already established. The pathway ahead seems clear. If your brain never established a path of trust, however, it might feel like walking into a jungle where there's no clear path. Even if a secure childhood established in your brain a path of trust, having our trust broken by another can disrupt the path. The bridge from you to other people gets damaged.

We could say that a breach of trust results, somewhat literally, in brain damage. Trusting another person when the trust system in your brain has been broken is like playing basketball on a broken ankle. Your ankle needs healing, not intense exercise. The way of rebuilding your bridge of trust is similar to how you built trust in the beginning. Trust starts by trusting someone just enough to talk about your life. Pastors, counselors, and spiritual directors can be safe people to begin with. When someone listens to you in a nonjudgmental, compassionate manner, your brain damage begins to heal.

In other words, even if the bridge of trust is utterly wiped away, your brain is capable of forming a new structure to allow you to trust others. Over time, as you allow yourself to be known by another person—even just one person—your trust bridge is rebuilt. Eventually you will be able to put your weight down on that bridge and trust others. Essentially, by forming a secure attachment with a loving, trustworthy person, we can receive what we either didn't get when we were young or what was disrupted at some point through a breach in trust.

When you're learning to trust others and God, you don't even need a brain surgeon to repair your brain. You just need a good, trustworthy listener.

REFLECTION QUESTIONS

1. What events have damaged your ability to trust people or God?

2. Who are some people in your life in whom you seek refuge? Do you seek refuge in God?

3. When have you felt heard and seen by another person?

4. What would it feel like to be heard and seen by God?

SPIRITUAL INTELLIGENCE PRACTICE: TRUST-BUILDING

This exercise will build your own ability to trust, and you will also be inviting another person to grow in trust as well. Find a conversation partner—a friend, your spouse, or a family member—with whom you can be honest. Set aside an hour. This might seem like a long time for one person to speak, but trust me: I've done this with groups, and the time usually flies by.

1. Decide who will share first. For the first thirty minutes, one person speaks, and the other person listens. When you are the speaker, share some way that your trust has been broken by another.

2. Then switch places for the second thirty minutes so the other person can share about a time that their trust has been broken.

3. At the end of the hour, pray for each other about the things that you each brought up.

PRAYER

O God, my deliverer, as I embark on this journey of faith and love, open the way in me for healing and growth. Make a way where there appears to be none. Replace my insecurity with trust in you that I may learn to attach my life to you above all other things and people. Let me receive your unfailing love. Let me be transformed by it, that your love may flow through my life into the world.

God, my trust was broken when _____.

God, I trust that I am being healed of my broken trust. Help me to trust you and your care of me in all the circumstances of my life. Amen.

2 | THE PATH OF COMMUNICATING WITH GOD

My friend Beth has a way of cutting right to the chase. She had had a rocky relationship with God over the years but not for a lack of effort. She had tried on faith in many colors, but nothing seemed to fit. One time I asked her what she thought about praying with other people. "Terrifying," she said. "It's the most intimate thing there is." Truer words were never spoken.

One day Beth called me in an anxious state. "Paul, can you tell me why some people have much, much harder lives than others?" I told her I wasn't sure I could answer that question. In fact, I dread the question; there is simply no good answer.

"But you're a *pastor*," she chided. "You're supposed to have an answer!"

I wish. It's a valid question—and among the most common that humans ask ourselves and God. Yet I sensed something else was going on with her.

I already knew that Beth had lost her parents at a young age. I knew that she has had more than her share of difficult relationships and that she struggled with anxiety and depression. It turned out that she had just gone through a breakup, found out she was pregnant, and shortly after that found out that she had lost the baby. During the procedure, they discovered cancer.

I sat there, stunned and silent. When I finally found some words, I said them. It isn't fair, I told her. In fact, it totally sucks.

There was silence. Then she asked, "Can we pray?" I knew how difficult it was for her to ask that question. I began to pray. I lifted her grief and her hurt and her anger. I asked for healing of her body and soul. I asked God to let her experience joy. At this point, she cut in with her own plea, "God, I would be satisfied with just not feeling miserable. You don't even have to make me feel happy. Just take away the misery. I'm fine with okay." Within her voice lay a bare-bones, honest expression of pain. It cut right into my heart, and I believe it cut into the heart of God as well.

Sometimes what we really need is to just know God's there.

LEARNING TO COMMUNICATE WITH GOD

At the heart of communication is communion: a deep sharing and receiving. Communion is an offering of oneself and the receiving of the offering of another. It's being with one another at a very deep level—which, as Beth said, can be terrifying. Our deepest desire is to connect with another, and yet we fear how vulnerable that makes us. Some level of trust must first be established. If we share ourselves, will we be safe? If we speak what is in our hearts, will we be laughed at? Will what is precious within us be respected and loved, or will it be mocked and rejected?

Trust—that is, a sense of safety—will allow you to take a further step down the path of relationship with another, whether it be another human or God. That further step is communication. Being heard by God can transform your ability to receive God's love and give you the security needed to love others in the same manner, which is your spiritual intelligence.

Our very first communication as babies may be the most effective and honest communication we will ever have: crying. In one of my first therapy sessions, I began to cry. I quickly tried to stifle my tears, and in so doing, I must have unconsciously closed my mouth. "No, Paul," my therapist said gently. "Keep your mouth wide open and let your tears come."

Can you imagine a baby with a mouth agape, crying? At some point, many of us learned to stop crying. My favorite saint, Mister Rogers, said, "People have said, 'Don't cry' to other people for years and years, and all it has ever meant is *I'm too uncomfortable when you show your feelings: Don't cry.*" To get to a deep level of communication with God—or anyone—we have to learn to cry out again.

As a coach and pastor, I find that when someone meets with me for the first time, they often cry. Perhaps it is because they haven't had someone to listen to them in a long time. They have stifled their tears. And so, naturally, tears are the first things to come. Communication is about sharing yourself—your fears, your hurts, your hopes—with another.

Two books in the Bible cover the life of Samuel, the prophet and judge of Israel. His mother, Hannah, had struggled to conceive, and she was miserable. Hannah's cries were not being heard, which is one of the worst feelings a human can have. Her husband dismissed her weeping about not having children, and her husband's other wife teased her mercilessly. Who would hear her with love and understanding?

She found her way to the temple of God and began to pour out her soul in sobs and unintelligible utterances. At least that's all the priest Eli could hear. He accused her of being drunk.

But God was hearing her loud and clear. She asked God to give her a child. To Eli's credit, when Hannah explained that she had been praying, Eli responded by showing that he was indeed now hearing her. Although he did not know what her plea to God was, he declared, "Go in peace; the God of Israel grants the petition you have made to him" (1 Sam 1:17). Hannah left with peace, and a new hope was born in her that she would conceive and deliver a child. When she did, she named him Samuel, which in Hebrew means "God has heard."

A TWO-WAY STREET

The originator of attachment theory, John Bowlby, began his research by observing infants at orphanages in post–World War II Europe. When the children first arrived, they would cry out desperately for their mothers. But eventually they would stop crying. Before Bowlby's research, the conventional wisdom had been that the babies had learned to self-soothe. But in fact, they had just resigned themselves to a reality without a mother. The babies grew into children and then adults who didn't ask for help and who were unable to fully trust others enough to get close to them.

We might cry out to God in a moment of desperation. But if we can never discern a response from God, our prayers will be infrequent. If we sense that God never responds to our cries for help, we will learn to resign ourselves to a reality without God. We may still say we "believe" in God. We may go to worship services and even enjoy the ritual or community. But do we expect that God will speak to us in some discernible way? Can you have a one-way relationship with God or anyone? How would you know if God responded to you?

It helps to have a mentor—someone to help identify for you what is God's voice and what is not. That might take the form of a spiritual director, or a friend, or a mentor, or a pastor.

The aged priest Eli became such a person for Hannah's son, Samuel. As promised, Hannah brought her son, Samuel, to be dedicated in the service of God at the temple. One night, young Samuel heard a voice calling his name. He assumed it was Eli, but Eli said it was not him and sent him back to bed. After a few times, Eli realized what was happening. "Go, lie down," he told Samuel, "and if he calls you, you shall say, 'Speak, Lord, for your servant is listening'" (1 Sam 3:9–10). Samuel did just that, and God began to speak.

Samuel became the next judge and prophet of Israel. The biblical writer tells us that the Lord was with him and let none of his words fall to the ground. Samuel became a great listener of God.

Perhaps you pray regularly to God. But have you ever asked God to speak to you?

PAYING ATTENTION

It had been a rough day. A year earlier, I had resigned as pastor of a church I loved because I felt called to coach and train ministry leaders. It was a huge risk, and it wasn't clear that it would work out. I started telling God that I was unhappy and afraid. Driving through town, I had worked up a pretty good set of tears. I honestly didn't even know what to ask God for, so I just said, "God, I need you to speak to me."

Something in my mind said, "Pay attention." I looked around and noticed that I was on Campbell Road. *Hmm.* Campbell is my daughter's name. I turned left and saw a restaurant named Nelson's Steakhouse. Nelson is my son's name. *Hmm.* Then I saw another restaurant named La Hacienda. It was the very place where my wife and I hosted our rehearsal dinner on the eve of our wedding. I began to wonder what God might be saying. This is what came into my mind:

"You remember, Paul, after you had failed at multiple relationships, you prayed for a wife who was healthy and loving. I gave you Jennifer. And do you remember that after ten years of praying to have biological children, you decided to adopt? I gave you Nelson. Then you prayed for a baby sister for Nelson, and I gave you Campbell. What makes you believe I will fail you now? Trust me."

Hearing God requires openness and attention. God comes in signs and thoughts and in any way that God can get into your consciousness. Listening will require imagination and faith. You have to give God a chance to speak and then be ready. It might not be immediate. It might take time. And you might have to talk with a trusted friend or mentor to figure out what it means.

Two weeks after Beth and I had prayed together, I got a text from her: "It happened." "What happened?" I asked. "God showed up." What? How? She told me that I might think she needed to be institutionalized. Now I was really intrigued.

She was walking her dog down a wooded path the previous evening when suddenly what must have been thousands of fireflies converged on her, enveloping her. It would have been a strange occurrence no matter what but especially when you consider that it was March. Fireflies didn't appear in her region of the country for at least another three months.

I asked her why she believed this was God showing up. She explained that the last time she had seen a firefly, she was a child at her grandparents' farm. "The last time I felt truly happy," she told me. Since that wonderful, wooded walk with God, whenever she sees fireflies, they remind her that God is there and cares.

ATTACHMENT STYLES

Based on your interactions with your caregivers as well as other environmental factors, you developed, in the first year of your life, a potentially lifelong pattern of relationship. This pattern is called your attachment style.

In the 1960s, psychologist Mary Ainsworth designed "The Strange Situation" experiment. Infants sat surrounded by toys and a chair where an adult could sit. Sometimes that adult was the baby's mother. But at different points the mother was removed from the room, and a stranger entered. Sometimes both the mother and the stranger were present. Ainsworth observed how the child responded to the mother coming and going, as well as their interactions with the stranger.

Out of these observations, Ainsworth saw four patterns emerging: (1) secure, (2) anxious or ambivalent, (3) avoidant or dismissive, and (4) fearful or disorganized.

Roughly 50–70 percent of the children appeared to have a **secure** attachment with their caregivers. When the mother was in the room, Ainsworth noted, they happily played with the toys and explored the room. When the mother left, they cried and searched for their mother. When *both* the mother and the stranger were in the room, they were more interested in their mother but not frightened by the presence of the stranger.

Children identified as demonstrating an **anxious** attachment style were more focused on their mothers than the toys. When the mother left, they were highly distressed. When the mother returned, they sought the mother, but they were still not comforted. Not only were they not comforted, but they often responded angrily to the mother, both clinging and pushing away. They were afraid of the stranger whether the mother was present or not.

Other children, identified as **avoidant** in attachment style, paid very little attention to their mother whether she was in the room or not. They played with their toys. When the mother returned, they either ignored her or moved away from her. They were fairly indifferent to the stranger if no less avoidant with them than with their mothers.

The final pattern that emerged is referred to as a **disorganized**, or fearful, attachment style. The reactions of these infants to their mothers were unpredictable but, overall, leaning toward showing fear. When the mother reentered the room to approach the child, they withdrew in fear. They showed distrust and fear to both mother and stranger.

These attachment styles remain consistent in our adult relationships. When we are secure, we can trust our partners and

SECURE
Receives love & trusts others. Gives and receives love freely.

ANXIOUS
See self as not worthy of being loved. Uses loves to get love. Chases love.

AVOIDANT
Sees others as not trustworthy. Pushes love away out of suspicion.

FEARFUL
Not worthy of love and distrusts others. Attacks or flees love.

friends and freely express ourselves to them. We can see ourselves as worthy of love and trust others to love us back. We are able to give and receive love more easily.

When we are anxious, we tend to see ourselves as not worthy of being loved. We try to please others so that they will love us. When our mates are not pleased, we feel rejected and respond with anger.

Those of us who are avoidant may value ourselves greatly but view others with distrust. In times of stress, we will tend to push others away and isolate ourselves.

Finally, those of us with a disorganized or fearful attachment style struggle to see our own value and to trust others. We have no real source of security, either within ourselves or other people. We may flee or attack our partners with little rhyme or reason. Our relationships are volatile and often short-lived.

Remember that attachment theory is all about how we behave in times of threat, grief, and loss. When we are not experiencing crisis, most of us are fully capable of having healthy relationships. It is when our security is shaken that we revert to our insecure patterns. We cling, we push, we isolate, we attack, we freeze, we flee. We become more like we were when we were babies, when our caregiver has left the room, or when a stranger has entered it.

ATTACHED TO GOD?

Spiritual intelligence is all about your ability to receive and give love. To have a healthy, loving relationship with God, self, and others, you must have an abiding sense of security. So the question becomes: How do you move from insecurity to security?

We go back to how secure attachment is formed in the beginning. Secure attachment forms when our primary attachment figure is nearby, accessible, and attentive. Counselors and pastors can be of great help in bringing about security, but they cannot go back in time to meet the requirements of being nearby, accessible, and attentive like a parent could be with a baby. Spouses can also help greatly; having a partner with a secure attachment style can very much contribute to your own sense of security. Yet to ask your partner to be your mother or father and reraise you is quite a burden to place on them. Also, not everyone has a partner with a secure attachment style. Or if we do, what happens when our partner dies?

When you put all of your security in something or someone that will die, what happens to your security when they do? How can you possibly find comfort when your only source of comfort is replaced by loss and grief? You can't.

Sometimes people talk about "reparenting yourself," which includes offering your younger self the attention and care you didn't receive as an infant or a child. That can be a helpful strategy. Yet as relational creatures, we are limited in the amount of comfort we can extend to ourselves.

We might find some help here in a sixteenth-century document. Stay with me here; I know this might feel like a stretch. The *Heidelberg Catechism* offers a series of questions and answers to all things in the Christian faith. The very first question is "What is your only comfort in life and in death?"

And here's the answer: "That I am not my own, but belong—body and soul, in life and in death—to my faithful Savior, Jesus Christ."

The answer continues:

He has fully paid for all my sins with his precious blood,
and has set me free from the tyranny of the devil.
He also watches over me in such a way
that not a hair can fall from my head
without the will of my Father in heaven;
in fact, all things must work together for my salvation.

Because I belong to him,
Christ, by his Holy Spirit,
assures me of eternal life
and makes me wholeheartedly willing and ready
from now on to live for him. (The Heidelberg Catechism Q. 1)

You may struggle to believe every word of this, and that's fine. I want you to pay attention not to the doctrine but to the language of attachment this ancient document contains: *comfort, belong, watches over, not a hair can fall from my head*. There is a deep and abiding security evoked here, one that comes from making Christ, or God, one's primary attachment figure. When crisis comes, we can seek God in addition to seeking support from others.

But what if we cannot find God? What if we pray and discern no response? The attachment cannot form—between child and parent, between a human and God—unless there is a two-way relationship. For the attachment to be real and vital, we must be able to discern God as nearby, accessible, and attentive.

Like a baby hears a mother's reassuring voice, we must be able to hear God—and not in a distant voice but nearby or even from within. God knows how to reach you if you are paying attention. God speaks through street signs and lightning bugs. The spiritual intelligence practice at the end of this chapter might help you name some of the ways God communicates with you.

So how can we sense God's presence? That is the pathway we will explore next.

REFLECTION QUESTIONS

1. What is one of the most bare-boned, honest prayers you have offered?

2. When was a time you felt certain that God heard your prayers?

3. Have you ever sensed God was trying to communicate with you?

4. What might you do to listen and watch for God in response to your prayers?

SPIRITUAL INTELLIGENCE PRACTICE: TWO-WAY COMMUNICATION WITH GOD

Remember the Being of love, goodness, and protection that you imagined at the beginning of chapter 1? Now, in your mind's eye, imagine the God who looks like that. Breathe deeply and imagine yourself in the presence of such a loving, good, protective God.

1. Tell God something you are afraid of or worry about.

2. Tell God something you hope for.

3. Thank God for things for which you are thankful.

4. Over the next week, identify three instances in which you believe God was communicating with you. Remember that God can communicate with us in many ways, including through words, images, emotions, signs, the natural world, and other people.

PRAYER

O God who hears and speaks, open me up to the real possibility of direct communication with you. Let me speak and know you hear me. Let me listen and know you speak to us.

God, the deepest cry of my heart today is _____.

Hear my prayer and reveal yourself to me in the coming week so that I may know that you are there and that you hear me. Amen.

3 | THE PATH OF SENSING GOD'S NEARNESS

Think of a mother hovering over a crib and scooping up her child to hold them. Her very presence provides comfort. When she holds the baby close, it gives the baby a sense of security. Secure attachment is being formed.

The three key ingredients for a secure attachment are that our caregivers are: (1) nearby, (2) accessible, and (3) attentive. John Bowlby, the pioneer of attachment theory, wrote, "When an individual is confident that an attachment figure will be available whenever they desire it, that person will be much less prone to either intense or chronic fear than will an individual who for any reason has no such confidence." Proximity with our caregivers greatly increased our sense of security. When there was trouble, we looked for a parent and made a beeline for them. Can an invisible God give us that same sense of security or perhaps even greater? What would it take to sense God's nearness?

Between the ages of four and seven months old, children develop what is called object permanence. By this age, children can conceptualize that objects or people still exist even when they cannot see them. This allows a baby to trust that a ball doesn't stop existing just because it is hidden by a blanket. It allows a child to spend the day at daycare and still believe that they will see their parents at the end of the day. Object permanence is the beginning of a more permanent sense of security. If a parent has shown themselves to be reliable in keeping their child safe, then the child can believe that they are safe even when Mom isn't nearby.

Perhaps this is the beginning of the ability to believe in an invisible God. When object permanence occurs, the brain facility has been established for such belief. In terms of spiritual intelligence, the nearer one perceives God to be, the less fearfully and more lovingly a person can respond to the world. Believing that God is ever present and able to respond to us when we are in need allows us to face grief, loss, and illness with security. With our sense of security intact, we can act courageously rather than being overtaken by fear, which causes us to fight, flee, or freeze. That's not to say we won't *feel* fear. It's just that we'll be able to return to a sense of security in the midst of it.

With spiritual intelligence, this ability to act courageously corresponds to the ability to love others in the manner that Christ loves. We can love selflessly and for the sake of the other person and not ourselves. We can love even at the risk of our own lives, which goes directly against our basic survival instincts. Love gives us courage.

GOD'S PRESENCE IN HUMAN FORM

A starting place for sensing God's presence is sensing God's presence through other humans.

As part of my training for ministry, I served as a chaplain for the maternity area of a hospital. While it was a great joy to offer blessings for healthy babies, most of my work was with mothers and fathers in very difficult and sometimes soul-crushing situations.

I remember my first encounter with a husband and wife who had just lost a child. The administrative assistant of pastoral care handed me a short note: "Fetal demise. Spanish only. Room 723." At that time, I had spent only one week in training, shadowing an experienced mentor. But she was out for the week, and so I was the only chaplain available.

I called a translator, and she met me outside the patient's room. I briefly described the scenario and that the couple had just learned of the loss of their child. We both gulped. She knew her role: translation, although most of what had happened needed no translation. But I wasn't sure I knew mine.

We entered the room, and I kind of ushered the translator inside in front of me. After all, the young couple needed some explanation of why I was there: not a doctor, not a nurse, but a chaplain. They send doctors and nurses to patients when there is hope of healing and recovery. They send in chaplains for the rest.

I will never forget the eyes of the helpless husband—big, scared eyes. His wife's face was ashen with grief, her eyes cast downward. He explained to me that this was their third experience of child loss. He was afraid that this was too much for his wife.

The translator's job was not easy. She had to repeat a difficult story of infant death; possibly, it was one she had heard before or even experienced herself. And my job wasn't either. It quickly became clear that no words of consolation or advice, in any language, would be even remotely helpful or appropriate. What could I possibly tell this couple about how to cope with this immense grief?

I feebly offered the only thing I had: prayer. The husband's eyes lit up as if to say, yes, please, that's what we need. So we all joined hands, including the translator, as I lifted up the couple's pain to God. I don't remember now what words I said, but I tried to talk to God as if God were right there in the room with us. Because I believe God was.

The woman was in tears. They were her first tears since learning that her baby had died. She began to talk now and make eye contact. It was as if the prayer had turned on a light. The healing had begun. It was only the beginning, as anyone who has experienced the loss of a child knows. The acute stages of grief can last a long, long time. But it was like the prayer had given the mother's grief a container—a place to put it.

As I was leaving, the husband walked after me and, in his best English, thanked me. He asked if I would come back to pray with them the next day. I had always known that prayer was important, but on that day, I learned how much people need it. The couple did not need my words or my presence. It was *God's* presence for which they had so desperately longed.

At times, God can seem so absent or so far away that we need a person in the flesh—even a nervous young chaplain—to represent God's presence. God's presence can be experienced in human form. Isn't that what Jesus is all about?

Jesus's disciples had spent the whole day with Jesus as he cured many who were sick. When it was late, rather than sending the people away to get food, Jesus told the disciples to feed them. There were thousands, and all they had were five loaves of bread and two fish. Miraculously, everyone received what they needed.

Miracles aside, serving five thousand households would be exhausting. Jesus then told the disciples to row to the other side of the lake while he prayed by himself. They toiled through the night against powerful wind and waves. Early in the morning, before dawn, there appeared a lone figure walking on the water. In their weary and wary frame of mind, they thought it must be a ghost and cried out in terror. Here's what Matthew writes: "But immediately Jesus spoke to them and said, 'Take heart, it is I; do not be afraid.' Peter answered him, 'Lord, if it is you, command me to come to you on the water.' He said, 'Come'" (Matt 14:27–28).

Peter had learned to rely on Jesus. Jesus had shown himself as someone Peter could trust. Jesus represented a secure attachment figure to Peter. He believed that if this really was Jesus, then he had nothing to fear. Jesus was near and would not lead him into harm.

So Peter did the impossible. He got out of the boat and began to walk toward Jesus. Imagine a child taking their first steps: their eyes are on their mother, and they believe they can do it because she is there encouraging them. Even if they fall, they will be okay, they think, because Mom is nearby.

Only when the waves and wind increased did Peter get distracted and begin to sink, crying out, "Lord, save me!" But

Jesus was right there to catch him. God in the flesh caught him.

When fear or insecurity overtakes us, we lose the ability to act courageously, which includes the ability to love others in the way of God. Sensing the presence of God can restore your courage.

HOW DO WE CULTIVATE AWARENESS OF GOD'S PRESENCE?

I grew up with a basic belief in God. I understood that there was a God and that this God interacted with human beings—at least in Bible times. But I am not sure I had experienced God's presence in a visceral way until I was in my late twenties.

I was reading *Mere Christianity* by Christian thinker C. S. Lewis. In that book, Lewis addresses our struggle to understand how God can tend to several hundred million human beings all praying at the same time. He presents an illustration of an author writing a novel of your life. An author does not live in the timeline of their own book. God, who exists outside of our earthly sense of time, has an eternity of time to spend with you. From one moment to the next, God might spend several millennia reflecting on that one moment.

As I read, I imagined God sitting in a vast library. God could pick up my book and be with just my story or anyone's story, I thought. Then I read these words of Lewis's: "He has infinite attention to spare for each one of us. He does not have to deal with us in the mass. You are as much alone with him as if you were the only being he had ever created."

In that moment, my mind was blown. It was like a view of the earth from space zoomed in on me, sitting there in my armchair. Suddenly, God was close. It was just us. No one else. God was in no hurry. That moment represented a radical change in my belief. God was no longer in the theoretical to me. God was real, and God was close. Very close.

In Psalm 139:7–10, David asks:

> Where can I go from your spirit?
> Or where can I flee from your presence?
> If I ascend to heaven, you are there;
> if I make my bed in Sheol, you are there.
> If I take the wings of the morning
> and settle at the farthest limits of the sea,
> even there your hand shall lead me,
> and your right hand shall hold me fast.

For David, God was ever present. He carried an awareness of God's presence with him throughout his day.

A visitor of the church I was serving once asked if she could speak with me. Jill sat down and said matter-of-factly, "I don't believe in God. But I think my life would be better if I did. Can you coach me on believing in God?"

I had spoken to many atheists and agnostics, and I knew that you cannot convince a person to believe in God no matter how well versed in theology or the Bible you are. But what about an atheist who longs to believe—and asks you for help?

I began by asking her questions. I asked her why she thought her life would be better if she believed in God. She told me she believed that such a faith would be a comfort to her in difficult times. I asked her about what difficult times she had experienced. The love of her life had died, she said, and what little faith she had left had died with him.

I asked Jill more about why she didn't believe in God. She explained that she was raised in a fundamentalist Christian family. Whether at church or home, she felt judged and ashamed. Then there was the history of Christianity, she said; it was filled with things like the Inquisition in Spain, the Crusades, forced conversions, and witch trials. Oh, and then there's the Bible, she added. What about the book of Joshua? God led Joshua and the Israelite army to destroy whole peoples in order to take the land of Canaan. How could she believe in such a God?

One more question popped into my mind. "What if none of those things existed?" I said. "No church. No Bible. No history. Just you and a Being that created you. What would you want that God to be like?"

Jill described a God who loved her just as she is. This God was forgiving, merciful, compassionate, and was with her and everyone else all the time. I said that I liked the sound of that God. Then I asked, "If there *were* such a God, where would you most likely experience that God?" She said that she loved to be out in nature. When her husband was alive, they often went to state parks and hiked on trails.

I told her that I would pray that God would meet her in nature as she walked. I would do the praying until she felt she could join me. But for now, I told her, just find a place outside to go for walks.

For a few months, we met and talked. I listened to her experience with grief and her observations on her walks. She walked. I prayed. Then one day I got an email from Jill. Something had happened. It was a gorgeous fall day, she told me, and she was walking in her favorite state park. She was marveling at the beautiful foliage of the trees that stand around a still lake when she noticed a dock jutting out into the water. On it stood a woman.

As Jill approached, the stranger had her back turned toward her, looking out on the lake. Then suddenly, the woman turned to my friend with a broad smile and said, "Isn't God amazing?"

Jill wrote that before she could think, the words just came out of her mouth: "Yes! Yes, he is!" Suddenly, she said, "And then God was everywhere. I couldn't *not* see God. God was being reflected all around."

It wasn't that God had suddenly appeared. It was that she could suddenly see.

YOUR BRAIN'S CONSCIOUSNESS CONTROLLER

Right now, your brain is sorting out what is relevant to pay attention to and what it can simply ignore. It can do this with 140 distinct pieces of data at a time. Your brain does this sorting so that it does not become overloaded with data processing. The part of your brain that does this sorting is called the reticular activating system (RAS). It's kind of like a relay switch. It controls your level of consciousness all the way down to deep sleep and up to high alert arousal. It seeks out what you have deemed most important in your environment. The default setting for your RAS is survival. What it deems most important are things that jeopardize your safety and things you need to survive.

Most stimuli in your environment—such as the temperature, assuming it's constant and comfortable—do not require your attention. Now if all of a sudden it starts getting hotter and hotter, then your RAS will begin to send signals to two places. One is your prefrontal cortex, which allows you to analyze the temperature situation. You might look around and see if other people appear hot. But unless you smell smoke, you will probably assume that the heat got turned up or it has warmed up outside. You're in no danger, but you might want to get a glass of water.

But before your RAS sends signals to your prefrontal cortex, it sends it to your amygdala, which is essentially your fear center and a more animalistic part of your brain. Any time your RAS recognizes something different or new in your environment, it alerts your amygdala, which prepares your body for action. Elevating your senses and sending adrenaline into your body, the signal to your amygdala prepares you to fight or run. The signal that goes to your prefrontal cortex—the conscious, thinking part of your brain—arrives later. In other words, you might *react* before you *think*. It's important, then, to give your brain time to analyze the situation before you react simply out of fear. All this happens in a split second.

So every time you hear something new that is in some way in opposition to what is familiar, your natural first response is one of fear. Your base, animal, instinctive response is to fight, run, or freeze. If there is a true threat, this response might save your life. But if there is not a true threat, and if you do not take time to investigate further with the thinking part of your brain, you might be fighting or running for no reason.

Curiosity is the best state of mind for learning and for relationships. Our brains are much more receptive to information from our environment—whether it be the person talking to us or something going on in the corner of our vision—when we are curious than when we are afraid. The better our fear centers are being held in check, the more we can perceive.

Jill's openness to perceiving God's presence paved the way for her encounter in the woods. Her past experiences with the church, the Bible, and her family of origin triggered fear in her, which had shut down her belief in God.

One of the unique features of our brains is that they do not allow us to see what we don't believe or can't understand. The RAS filters these things out. Seeing something that we cannot conceive of or believe in would be like listening to static on a radio. We just turn to a station that we get.

A simple way to understand the RAS is what has been dubbed the yellow car phenomenon. Once a person learns a new word or concept, they begin to see it more frequently. It is no longer static, but something is recognizable. Have you noticed that when you buy a new car, you begin to see that make, model, and color everywhere? Did everyone in your neighborhood suddenly go out and buy the same yellow car? No. It is just that your brain has now judged that yellow cars are important to you, and so you see yellow cars all the time now.

In your default mode, your brain is looking for danger. In fear mode, your brain shuts out things that don't pose a threat or are not necessary for your survival. But what if you began to inform your brain that there are more aspects of life than just survival? What if you were on the lookout for acts of kindness instead of acts of violence? What if you were on the lookout for God?

By changing your focus, you will change what you see. Rather than being on guard all the time, you will begin to approach the world with a curious mindset, open to new possibilities—even open to witnessing God at work in the world.

In this sense, faith becomes a matter of shifting what you are paying attention to. Jill shifted her attention from the abusiveness of Christians of her past to looking for a God that loved her just the way she is. It was as if God became a yellow car. God was everywhere now.

Sometimes even believing in the *possibility* of God will be enough to see God. And what if, like David, you believed God saw you back? What if God loved you and wanted to be with you and speak with you and help you? Would you be curious enough to set your brain's consciousness controls to look for this God?

EXPERIENCE BUILDS BELIEF

One of the questions I like to ask people who seek to grow in their faith is this: "When was a time you suspected God was real?" Many people can point to an experience where it seemed that God had shown up for them. It is usually in a time of crisis: their grandmother was dying, they were just diagnosed with cancer, or they were in some kind of danger.

These are the moments on which we build our faith. Yes, perhaps we believed that the Bible is true or God exists because our parents told us so. But true faith comes with an experience with God.

The more we believe, the more we experience; the more we experience, the more we believe. It is an upward spiral of faith. For some people, God showed up out of nowhere, and then they believed. Others sought out God with just an inkling of hope, and when they found God, their belief was confirmed.

Your openness and your attention are your best tools for growing your faith. Over time, your experience of God will become as frequent as your willingness to become aware of God. We all get lost in the fears and worries of the world. We lose sight of God. We go back into our human default mode of survival. That is why building practices that remind us of God's presence is so important.

This is not a book about spiritual practices; there are many good ones out there that friends or a pastor or a spiritual director can recommend. We can pray, read the Bible, memorize Scripture, go to church, or spend time in God's creation. For Jill, just going for a walk and paying attention changed everything.

What we pay attention to the most deeply will be the thing we see the most frequently. What if we, along with Jill, began opening ourselves to the possibility of seeing God?

REFLECTION QUESTIONS

1. When you were a child, in what ways did you feel safe or unsafe?

2. An attachment figure is someone you turn to in times of crisis. Who are your attachment figures now?

3. Was there a time in your life when you felt that God was not there for you?

4. When was a time when you felt that God was with you?

SPIRITUAL INTELLIGENCE PRACTICE: PSALM 139

Find Psalm 139 in any Scripture translation that you like. This exercise has you encountering the psalm in a variety of ways. Be creative by interacting with the psalm in different ways. Every time you see 139, you could remember that God is with you. Or you could find a two-part phrase that jumps out at you and use it as a short breath prayer—saying one phrase as you inhale, and another phrase as you exhale.

1. Recite the psalm as a prayer every day this coming week. Imagine Christ sitting in front of you as you pray.

2. After the reading, say whatever else you would say to Christ if you were face to face with him.

3. At the end of the week, write a letter from Christ to you. Write whatever you believe he would say to you if he were face to face with you.

PRAYER

O Loving Parent, you hear me, you see me, and you come to me. You are with me day and night, in the good times and the hard times. Awaken me to your presence as I seek to know you more deeply.

God, be with me as I _____.

God, help me to feel safe with you at all times. Give me the courage to grow in loving you, myself, and others. Amen.

Part II

SELF-DIFFERENTIATION:
BECOMING FREE TO BE YOURSELF

4 | THE PATH OF FORGIVENESS

The three paths we've traveled thus far—the paths of trusting God, communicating with God, and sensing God's nearness—help us find secure attachment with the Being who created us. We turn now to the work of self-differentiation—the capacity to feel and think for ourselves rather than take on the feelings and thoughts of others—and the three pathways that help us become self-differentiated individuals.

The first is the hardest: forgiveness. In fact, when I lead groups through the process in this book, the most difficult session is inevitably this one. Those who struggle with receiving forgiveness for *themselves* feel shame and guilt more intensely when they talk about it. In fact, it often shuts them down. Those who struggle with forgiving *others* feel their hurt and anger more intensely. They may even direct their anger toward me for suggesting that forgiveness may be a necessary path.

So if you are feeling a variety of emotions you would rather not feel as you begin this chapter, you're not alone. You may want to skip this chapter. You may not be ready for this path. You can come back to it later.

But sooner or later, I believe we all have to address our forgiveness issues. Unforgiveness is like a clogged sink. God's love cannot flow through you if unforgiveness is clogging your soul. You must remove the clogs in order to have healthy, loving relationships with God, self, and others.

Let's be clear: God's attachment to *us* can never, ever be broken. But blockages can keep God's loving life from penetrating deeply and producing healthy, life-giving love in us.

Self-differentiation is the ability to distinguish between our own thoughts and feelings and the thoughts and feelings of others. Forgiveness is part of what gives us the ability to separate ourselves from others. Otherwise, we remain unhealthily and harmfully bound to our offenders. Self-differentiation is about becoming free from the control of others or the need to control others so that we can be free to be who God created us to be.

Forgiveness is one of the keys to spiritual intelligence, our capacity to have loving relationships with God, ourselves, and the world. We can use that power to forgive ourselves; after all, we are already forgiven by God for everything we have done or will do. You might think of forgiveness as a salve. It won't do much good remaining in the jar; you have to use it. You can rub it on your own broken places, and you can offer it to others.

If you are satisfied with your life the way it is, then forgiveness serves no purpose. The thing that leads people to seek the path of forgiveness is dissatisfaction.

WHY DO WE NEED FORGIVENESS?

Before we talk more about forgiveness, let's examine why we need it. Whether you consider yourself a Christian or not, we likely agree that all human beings have a fundamental need to connect with others. This need to connect is what we call *attachment*. We need relationships to survive. But even beyond survival, we need relationships to be fulfilled as human beings.

In the previous three chapters, we looked at how a relationship with a loving, personal God gives us the security we need to cope with crises and develop into the people that God intended us to be. Given such a view of God, if we look at forgiveness as the thing we need merely to avoid punishment for breaking God's laws—well, we miss the point entirely.

When Jesus was asked which is the greatest commandment in the Law, he replied, "'Love the Lord your God with all your heart and with all your soul and with all your mind.' This is the first and greatest commandment. And the second is like it: 'Love your neighbor as yourself.' On these two commandments hang all the Law and the Prophets" (Matt 22:37–40).

The writers of the Hebrew Scriptures gave us guidelines for how to have loving relationships with God, yourself, and others. I include loving yourself because if we are to love our neighbors as ourselves, then learning to love ourselves is essential.

Biblical scholar William Barclay writes, "Sin is not so much the breaking of God's law but the breaking of God's heart." Sin is that which breaks hearts. It breaks relationships. It can be a breaking of our relationship with God, with other people, or even with ourselves. It is relationship damage—the kind of damage that leads us to insecurity in our relationships and blocks the flow of love.

Sin leads us to an impaired sense of the three outcomes of secure attachment. Those three outcomes that Bowlby referred to, again, are a sense of self-worth, a belief in the helpfulness of others, and a favorable model on which to build future relationships.

First, sin results in a poor sense of self-worth. In other words, we have a hard time believing we are worthy of being loved, including by God. In addition, sin makes us struggle to believe in the helpfulness of others, and this also includes the help given by God. We find it difficult to trust the God who says in Christ, "Come to me all of you who are weary and heavy burdened and I will give you rest" (Matt 11:28). Third, sin gives us a less favorable model on which to build future relationships. Our models of relationship are built on the model we were raised in, for better and for worse. We are all in need of a more loving foundation on which to build our relationships. We all need a new model.

God is the source of our love. When we attach our lives to God, we become attached to the source of love. Imagine a water hose unattached to the spigot. It isn't good for anything except to trip over in the yard. But when we attach it to the source of water, it can be used to nurture a whole garden.

Sometimes a hose gets a kink in it, and that constricted area blocks the flow of water. Sin is a kink in our hoses. It is the thing that keeps God's love from flowing through us into the world. The whole point of our lives is to water this world with God's love. Forgiveness unkinks your soul so that God's love can flow through you.

WHAT IS FORGIVENESS?

To attach to God—to rely on God above all other things—we must let go of other things that have caused us or others harm. Imagine hanging on to a vine on the side of a cliff. You can't let go unless you have something else to hold on to. Now imagine that a rope descends from the top of the cliff. To grasp it, you must let go of the vine. Christ is the rope, and he is securely attached to God at the top. The vine is everything that is not God that we have been using to survive in this life.

There is a Greek word in the New Testament that means to let go: *aphiemi*. It is generally translated as "forgive." To forgive means to "let go of" or to "set free." In order to let go of something or someone, we forgive. In a financial sense, to forgive is to release a person's debt. It could also be used for divorce: I release you from this marriage. Forgiveness does not have to lead to reconciliation. In fact, it gives us the freedom to decide the best path forward in our relationships. Forgiveness is letting go of our desire for punishment—punishment for others or for ourselves. It is letting go of anger, resentment, shame, guilt, and any number of feelings that block the flow of love. Forgiveness is not letting someone else off the hook for their sins. It is letting *yourself* off the hook from the sin of the world—including your own.

Forgiveness is not the same as reconciliation. Forgiveness is not submitting yourself to ongoing harm. Forgiveness is not forgetting. Forgiveness is not foregoing the pursuit of justice for your offender or the injustice of the world. Forgiveness is not weakness. Forgiveness restores your freedom from the offender and frees you to begin to heal.

After he had been raised from the dead, Jesus said to his disciples, "If you forgive the sins of any, they are forgiven them; if you retain the sins of any, they are retained" (John 20:23). Jesus gave his disciples a great gift: the power to forgive. Jesus still gives you and me the power to forgive. Besides love, it is the greatest power we have as human beings because it makes the way for love.

To have any relationship, you have to learn to forgive and to ask for forgiveness. In this model of spiritual intelligence, forgiveness is the first step in self-differentiation, which is our ability to separate ourselves from others' influences to become the people God called us to be. Forgiveness frees our true, God-given selves from the captivity of the world—from the sin and character of the world. Our souls are imprisoned by the world until we are set free through forgiveness.

UNFORGIVENESS PARALYZES US

Jesus was in his home base, teaching in a house. It was so crowded that no one else could get in. Four friends of a man who was paralyzed were so desperate to get their friend to the healer that they dug through the roof and lowered their friend down to Jesus. But that wasn't the most shocking thing that happened. When Jesus saw they had faith that their friend could be healed, he said a very surprising thing: "Son, your sins are forgiven" (Mark 2:5).

In Jesus's place and time, people assumed that if a person had a medical issue, it was a result of sin. It could even be the sin of the parents. So Jesus cut right to the assumed root cause: a need for forgiveness. The man was paralyzed with the belief that sin was the source of his paralysis. In order to be healed, he would first have to believe he was forgiven.

When we lack forgiveness, we are emotionally and spiritually paralyzed; we are frozen in a state of arrested development. This false belief—that we or others are beyond forgiving—blocks our ability to receive and give love. We either believe *we* don't deserve to be loved, or else we believe that other people don't deserve our love.

A lack of forgiveness can actually harm our physical health. Dr. Karen Swartz of Johns Hopkins School of Medicine writes, "There is an enormous physical burden to being hurt and disappointed." The anger that can result, she says, impacts our heart rate, blood pressure, and immune response. It can increase our risk of depression, heart disease, and diabetes. Conversely, forgiveness can actually calm our stress levels and lead to improved health. Forgiveness positively impacts our emotional, physical, and relational health. Without it, our health is at risk.

Forgiveness—or lack thereof—also impacts our relationship with God. Jesus said, "Forgive, and you will be forgiven. . . . But if you do not forgive others their sins, your Father will not forgive your sins" (Matt 6:14–15).

When you take Jesus at his word, it is hard to deny that there is a condition to receiving God's forgiveness. Still, without God's forgiveness, our relationship will be distant, just like any relationship where there is no forgiveness. To have a loving, intimate relationship with God, we must be willing to forgive others.

Forgiveness makes the way for love to flow in relationship. If the most important thing about being a child of God is to love God and to love our neighbors as ourselves, then we need forgiveness. And we need it in all dimensions: forgiveness from God, forgiveness for others, and forgiveness for ourselves.

Is forgiveness even possible for us? Some of the religious leaders present were appalled at Jesus's words. Forgiveness belonged to God alone, in their understanding. So for Jesus to declare this man forgiven meant he was either declaring that *he* was God or else that he was making an unauthorized use of God's powers. Either way, it was considered blasphemous.

Jesus responded by saying, "Which is easier, to say to the paralytic, 'Your sins are forgiven,' or to say, 'Stand up and take your mat and walk'? But so that you may know that the Son of Man has authority on earth to forgive sins," he said to the paralytic, "I say to you, stand up, take your mat and go to your home." And he stood up, and immediately took the mat, and went out before all of them so that they were all amazed and glorified God, saying, "We have never seen anything like this!" (Mark 2:1–12).

The Son of Man has the authority to forgive sins. *The Son of Man* is how Jesus often refers to himself; it was also a title associated with the Jewish messiah. But could it also mean *people* born of man—that is, all of humankind? Could he be referring to you? To me? Jesus gave his disciples the power to forgive.

REPENT AND RETURN

When someone tells me that they keep repeating the same relationship cycles, I begin to look for a need for forgiveness—something that needs letting go. Life has a way of returning us to the same problems over and over again until we make a change.

Perhaps the most misunderstood word in the Bible is *repent*. Our ears have been trained to hear it negatively. It often gets used to mean feeling sorrow for your sins. That is because the English translations of both the Hebrew and Greek words for repent have been filtered through a Latin word that shares the same root as *peni*tence. It generally means sorrow for one's sins.

But the ancient root of *repent* actually means "missing" or "to lack." The Greek word in the New Testament translated as "repent," used by Jesus, John the Baptist, and others, is *metanoia*, "to change one's way of thinking." In Hebrew, the word for "repent" is *teshuvah*, which means "to return." Repentance, then, is to return to God and to change the way you think. Thinking differently requires attachment to God rather than attachment to harmful ways of thinking and acting. We won't even want change unless we are truly dissatisfied with the way things are.

You may be miserable, or you may just have a sense that you lack something—something is missing from your life. Robert Quinn, an expert on organizational leadership, wrote a book entitled *Deep Change: Discovering the Leader Within*. The opening section is entitled "Deep Change or Slow Death." So many people and organizations choose a slow death over a meaningful change.

It's a sad reality. Perhaps the people to be pitied the most in this world are those whose lives are not that bad. Not good but not bad enough to seek a better life. They are choosing a slow death.

I was twenty-two years old and newly married but not to the woman I have been married to for over two decades now. There were good moments, but there was a lot of misery. We made each other miserable. It was slowly but surely killing us. I remember talking to my mom after a big fight my wife and I just had. "Paul, marriage is hard," my mother said, "but it's not supposed to be *this* hard." I had resigned myself to this life. One day I came home to find a moving truck. Much later, I learned that my former wife left for my sake. She knew that because of my beliefs about divorce, I would never end it. It turns out that leaving me was the most loving thing she could have done.

I eventually began to recognize a pattern that characterized all my romantic relationships and the part I had played in them. I never wanted to repeat this cycle again. I wanted to change. I began with reestablishing a life oriented around a relationship with God. I found a church and a pastor to talk with. That pastor assured me that God had forgiven me and wanted a better life for me. I had to want it too. I made new friends who were attempting to walk down the same path of relationship with God. I began to examine myself intensely, trying to understand what led to my failures. I needed to learn who I was and what I wanted and valued.

Is there something in your life that is slowly killing you? If so, is it time for a deep change? Perhaps it is time for you to self-differentiate.

I returned, I changed, I repented. This cycle is replacing my old cycles. I am beating a new path in my mind—a new way of thinking and living. I continue to return, change, repent. Little by little, I am becoming the me that God created me to be, which can only happen in a securely attached relationship with God.

The most important thing I had to do was to forgive—my former wife and the women before her, yes, but also myself for the part that I played. Today, when I think of my former loves, I only remember the love. I wish them well always. I am free from any resentment or regret—free to the degree that I have forgiven. This freedom is what makes the way for loving my wife today.

And incidentally, if you don't believe that people change, then you need to get to know some recovering alcoholics. I know several. One of my friends has been in recovery for over thirty years. He told me that as a young drunk man, a Texas judge declared him "incorrigibly alcoholic" and tossed him into the state penitentiary—yes, think of *penitence*, a related word. He had nearly killed a man in a bar fight. My friend discovered Alcoholics Anonymous and the twelve steps—which include surrendering your life to a higher power and the practice of forgiveness. Today he is a retired pastor.

If a Texas-sized, "incorrigible" murderous drunk can go for thirty years and counting without having a drink—well, then, there is nothing you can't change in your life, nothing that can't be forgiven with God's help.

RECEIVING FORGIVENESS

Forgiveness is a path toward self-differentiation, yes. But we could also call it the key to unlocking your spiritual intelligence—again, the degree to which we can receive God's love for ourselves and share it with others. When you can receive and give forgiveness, your relationships with God, self, and others all open into deeper, more loving levels.

It starts with receiving forgiveness for yourself. If you do not fully accept that God accepts you as you are, then accepting yourself may be a great challenge. This lack of self-acceptance results in the lack of acceptance of others. As the Scripture says, "Love your neighbor as yourselves." It is a command, but it is also a truth—a prescription and a description. We love our neighbors as ourselves. If we do not love ourselves, we will not love our neighbors well. And for us to love people, we must accept them. We can't love people where they *aren't*, only where they *are*. The same applies to us. We can only love ourselves truly as we are right now, not as we hope to be. The things we don't accept about ourselves lead us to not accept those same things about others.

Several years ago, I realized that I was judging people who struggled with their weight. Only after some reflection did I land on the deeper realization that I was ashamed of my own body. My struggle with judging others was really a lack of self-acceptance. The shame of self tends to be expressed as the judgment of others. Judgment shuts down our love. In her book *The Body Is Not an Apology: The Power of Radical Self-Love*, Sonya Renee Taylor writes, "How we value and honor our own bodies impacts how we value and honor the bodies of others." Learning to love and accept yourself, including your body, is key to loving and accepting others.

One of the key test items in my spiritual intelligence assessment, the GPS Spiritual Inventory, is to what degree you agree with the statement "I know that I am a work in progress and love myself as I am right now." Testers who score low on this question tend to score low on empathy too. They are related. If you can see yourself as a work in progress and love yourself as you are right now—not just when you get to the perfect weight—you will be able to see others as works in progress and love them as *they* are right now.

So how do we get to a place of self-acceptance? You have to stop judging and condemning yourself for not being perfect. Doing so decreases your self-empathy. Judgment and condemnation shut down the parts of our brains that allow for empathy to happen.

Self-empathy, sometimes called self-compassion, is the pathway that love travels. If the road is closed, love cannot travel. But how do we stop judging and condemning ourselves? We must learn to forgive ourselves. Yes, God has already forgiven us, but we have to take what God has given us and apply it to ourselves. Regularly.

Consider writing down everything you don't like about yourself. Then look yourself in the mirror and say, "I forgive you for . . ." Forgiveness is a practice. It takes time. Try to listen to the way you talk to yourself. Learn to speak to yourself as if you are someone you deeply love. Do not say anything to yourself that you wouldn't say to your spouse or children or anyone entrusted to your care.

THREE STEPS OF FORGIVING OTHERS

Forgiveness means letting go; sounds easy, right? You hear people say it all the time: "Just let it go!" But the path of forgiveness is, hands down, the hardest of the nine paths.

So why is letting go so hard? It is because the pain, fear, or disappointment caused by the offense remains. There is a need that has not been met and healing to be experienced. There is security that needs to be restored. We relied on someone, and they let us down. We still have needs that we count on others to provide.

I use a three-step pattern of forgiveness for myself and for my clients and parishioners: lean in, let go, let love flow. You could think of it as three beats: lean in, let go, let love. Before we can let go of what was done to us or what we have done to others, we must lean into our security system. This is how we get what we need and what helps us find security again. Then we are in a better place to let go. When we let go, this unclogs our hearts so that love can flow again.

Anytime you are feeling the symptoms of your unforgiveness, it's time to return to the three beats. Your symptoms may be anger, resentment, disappointment, anxiety, depression, self-harm, overeating, abusing alcohol, or any number of negative feelings and activities. When you identify these symptoms, try these things.

Lean into the relationships that help you to feel loved and restore your sense of trust. Turn to God, a partner, a friend, a counselor, a pastor, a parent. Lean into them. Tell them how you are feeling. Tell them what you need. Lean into healthy activities that stabilize your sense of well-being such as cultivating gratitude, doing meditation, exercising, going to church, or attending a twelve-step meeting.

Once you are feeling secure, you will be in a much better frame of mind to let go. So how do you let go? Think of your thoughts and feelings around the harm as an infected wound. It's one thing to have a wound, but lack of forgiveness is like a wound that has become infected. You need to express the infection. Say how you feel. Ideally, express yourself to the person you have harmed or who has harmed you. Express your sorrow and regret to the person you have harmed. To the person who has harmed you, tell them how what they did hurt you. This is assuming that you are safe in their presence. They may not forgive you. Or they may not apologize. But you still get the infection out of your system.

If you do not feel it is safe to have contact with the person or if the person has died, you will need a different tactic. Write a letter to the person expressing how you feel. You might even write a letter back from the person in response. You will have to use your imagination. If the person is dead or you are unable to speak directly with them, you could do the same thing out loud to an empty chair or with a counselor or friend who can stand in for the other person.

During the summer I spent working as a chaplain at a hospital, I got a call from the head nurse of palliative care. She told me that a man dying of cancer was having a hard time letting go. He was very angry. And also he did not believe in God.

I found him gaunt, pale, and withdrawn. I wondered if my presence might make him angrier. At first, that was true. He said, "No thanks, Chaplain. I don't want whatever you have to offer me." He seemed quite willing to express himself, however, and so I said I would just listen to whatever he had to say.

I asked him what he was angry about. He told me that his father had died six years earlier but that he hadn't spoken to him in the twenty years before that. They had had a difficult relationship, and after what seemed like the millionth fight, he had decided he didn't want to see his dad again. He felt judged and unloved.

I asked him if he grieved when his dad died, and he said that he didn't even shed a tear. After listening some more, I wondered what I had to offer him. Then an idea popped into my mind. "I know you don't believe in God or heaven, but I have a hypothetical question for you," I said. "If you died today and the first person you saw was your dad, what would you say?"

It was like a door opened in his soul—a place for all his feelings to flow through. All his hurt came out very suddenly. His eyes overflowed with tears and he said, "I love you, Dad!"

He didn't say, "I forgive you." But it was clear to me that the forgiveness happened as he said he loved him. He leaned into his own imagination, and perhaps even a bit of faith, to conjure an image of his dad.

Remember how a baby eventually learns object permanence? In some ways, that dying man was relearning the same thing a child learns when their mom leaves the room. He imagined his dad, and he was as good as there. He leaned into his grief and his forgiveness, and he let go, and he let love flow. He died later that day, and I believe he died full of love.

REFLECTION QUESTIONS

1. Jesus gave his disciples the power to forgive others. Hypothetically, if you had the power to forgive everyone who ever lived of everything, would you? Why or why not?

2. What is an example of unforgiveness that has paralyzed you or kept you from moving forward in your life?

3. What are some ways people have harmed you?

4. What harm do you feel called to forgive (let go of) at this time?

SPIRITUAL INTELLIGENCE EXERCISE: THE FORGIVENESS SNOWBALL

Here is an exercise in letting go. It helps you to name specific offenses—and offenders—and to practice forgiving each one. With each forgiveness, you will gain emotional energy and courage to forgive the next larger offense. It's a bit like a snowball rolling downhill. By the time you reach the big hurts, the momentum will help carry you through.

It's important to note here that when you speak these words, you aren't saying you will forget the harm or move back into relationship with the person. I am also not suggesting that forgiveness is a once-and-done practice. We may need to make the forgiveness snowball over and over again. But speaking forgiveness sets an intention to let go, and it gets us started on the forgiveness path.

1. Make a list of all the people you hold resentment against, including yourself. This could include people you don't even know personally, like public figures and sports stars.

2. Start by forgiving the smaller resentments like the people who cut you off in traffic or were rude to you at the grocery store. Simply say in your heart or directly to the person, "I forgive you for _____. And now I wish you well."

3. Move on to speaking forgiveness for the deeper and more difficult harms you have experienced.

4. If it is someone you know personally, consider reaching out to them if you feel so led.

PRAYER

Forgiving God, I carry heavy burdens of guilt, anger, and resentment. Free me to love as you love. Open me up to the possibility of living a forgiven and forgiving life. Help me to forgive others and myself. Give me the power, the will, and the opportunity to forgive.

O Lord, help me to forgive_____.

God who died in human flesh to forgive, let me be free from the harm that I have experienced or done to others. Amen.

5 | THE PATH OF EMOTIONAL REGULATION

I am not above bribery. I had promised my kids an outing to a pizza and arcade restaurant if they behaved well while their mother was out of town. When one of us is away, the other parent focuses on survival.

When my kids and I got to the restaurant, I ordered them a pizza and two forty-five-minute cards for the arcade. The kids would have to eat before they played because the forty-five-minute clock would begin when they played their first game. So we sat and waited for our square buzzer to go off.

We waited and waited. After twenty minutes, I approached the counter and asked if our food was almost done. "We haven't even started it. We have several orders in front of yours," the hurried and harried fellow behind the counter said. "I'm the only cook."

This last sentence would have aroused a better person's compassion, but the first two aroused my anger. They hadn't even *started* our order? Compassion never stood a chance. I raised my voice and said something about that not being my problem, and that we were leaving, and that I wanted a full refund, and that we were never coming back. My children stood silently as I fumed and crushed their well-earned reward.

Later that night, my son was struggling to fall asleep, and he said sadly, "Dad, I can't stop thinking of that man you yelled at. You were mean to him."

I felt horrible. That night, I had been anything but loving and Christlike. My emotions, run amok, had caused harm.

Perhaps you can relate. Do you remember the exercise at the end of the introduction? Finish this sentence: I can love others except when I_____. If you did the exercise then, find your list now. If you didn't do it, take a bit of time to do it now.

Here are a few of my answers, and apparently I should add "am at a pizza and arcade restaurant with my children and the food doesn't come":

- am frustrated

- am in a bad mood

- lose my temper

- discover things aren't going the way I planned

- am impatient, in a hurry

- find that something I value is being criticized

- don't get what I want

- am feeling threatened

Now note how many of your answers—and mine—involve emotions. Emotions, if left unchecked, can actually shut down your ability to love others.

The battle between love and survival instincts is fought on the field of emotions. Emotion, according to *Merriam-Webster*, is "a conscious mental reaction (such as anger or fear) subjectively experienced as strong feeling usually directed toward a specific object and typically accompanied by physiological and behavioral changes in the body." Emotion is an internal reaction to external forces. Emotion has a social element too; it is something we experience in relationship with people and our environment. Emotions are raw and organic. They just happen.

Feelings are more refined. They are shaped by emotions, thoughts, experiences, perspectives, and prejudices. Feelings persist, while emotions come and go based on circumstances and our relationships.

Emotions are cause and effect; there is motion in emotion. Something happens that impacts us, and it stirs physical feelings from within. It may quicken your heart rate and cause adrenaline to rush through your body. If you do not become aware of why you are feeling the way you do, then the motion will continue into your next interactions. It's like a domino effect. You get knocked down, and then you knock down the next person. Your boss yells at you, you come home and yell at your spouse, your spouse yells at your child, your child yells at the dog, the dog hides under the bed.

Both negative and positive emotions can spread. One afternoon, I was in the drive-thru line at a local fast-food joint. As I held out my debit card to pay, the cashier said with a contagious smile, "The person in front of you paid for your breakfast. What's crazy is that it started three cars in front of her!" I gladly passed on the joy and paid for the next person.

Who knows how long that line of generosity lasted? But for those of us who experienced the kind act of the first person that set it in motion, it changed our day. We probably all told that story to several people, and even sharing such a story gives people joy.

Unfortunately, studies show that negative emotions are more contagious than positive ones. The default setting of humans is geared toward survival, not sharing. Our seemingly instinctual emotional setting is much more attuned and reactive to things that threaten us than to things that inspire us. Uncontrolled anger or fear can spread like wildfire through a family, a church, a workplace, or even the whole world.

When I bring up the subject of emotional regulation, people often assume I mean that I am telling them to suppress emotions. Perhaps they imagine Mr. Spock. The *Star Trek* character, half-Vulcan and half-human, always appears unemotional, unaffected by the environment. Logic always rules his thinking and behavior. While I appreciate Spock—and I'd have been happy to have Spock go up to the counter for me that evening at the restaurant—he is not my model of how to be a healthy, loving human being.

Jesus is my model and the model for spiritual intelligence. We are talking about how a person becomes a child of God not just in name but in character. Jesus is the model for what it means to be fully human. In his life we see the true character of a child of God, and this includes the experience of emotions.

Spiritual intelligence starts with the concept of emotional intelligence. The *Oxford Languages Dictionary* defines emotional intelligence most concisely as "the capacity to be aware of, control, and express one's emotions, and to handle interpersonal relationships judiciously and empathetically." We can break this definition into two parts: (1) the capacity to be aware of, control, and express one's emotions and (2) the capacity to handle interpersonal relationships judiciously and empathetically and—I would add—lovingly. We will look at the second part of the emotional intelligence in the third part of this book. I would call the first part—the capacity to be aware of, control, and express one's emotions—emotional regulation.

Let's get something clear: emotional regulation is *not* the suppression of emotions. Emotions are a valuable and essential part of human existence. At the very least, emotion provides important data about what is going on in our environment and within ourselves. At its best, emotion takes us to the heights of human experience. What would giving birth to a baby be like without emotion? I imagine it would just be painful. With emotion, it is one of the most joyful experiences available on earth—though also painful, from what I am told.

The problem with a *lack* of emotional regulation is that emotions can overtake our ability to think, discern, love, and relate. Out-of-control emotions make us more like wild animals than loving human beings. In fact, the whole concept of emotional intelligence, when it emerged, challenged the idea that the main predictor for career success is IQ. Emotional intelligence ends up being a far greater predictor of success than IQ because the ability to navigate relationships is an invaluable skill in the corporate world. In God's world, relationships are everything.

For truly loving relationships to happen, we will need to walk down what feels like the scariest of paths: vulnerability, which we will turn to in the next chapter.

HARNESSING YOUR EMOTIONS

Emotional regulation, in this model of spiritual intelligence, is the capacity to be aware of, control, and express one's emotions lovingly. You might wonder, "How could one express anger lovingly?" Anger is an emotion that shows us what we value—what we have a deep attachment to. When something we are attached to—like a child or a spouse or a belief system—is threatened or demeaned in some way, anger might be the most natural emotion. Yet if we don't realize the source of our anger, we might just respond to the threat with a threat of our own. We might even respond with violence. It might seem a strange thing for our love for another to result in violence toward another, but it happens all the time.

Your anger probably doesn't often lead to violence, but it might lead you to harm a relationship. It might lead you to insult a person or to feel resentment that causes you to withdraw from relationship with them.

What would a loving expression of anger look like? It begins with awareness. Anger emerges as a sensation. A common figure of speech is "That really makes my blood boil." Our emotional state heats up. We may even clench our fists as if we are about to fight. Becoming aware that you are angry and naming it is a great first step toward a loving response. Awareness cuts the destructive version of anger off at the pass. The discerning part of your brain—the part that also includes your capacity to love—gets engaged. Just by thinking to yourself, *I'm angry*, a shift begins to happen from the more survival-oriented parts of your brain to the part of your brain where wise and loving choices can be made.

There is a deep level of awareness, one that you might have to access and reflect on at a later time. You can often find that deeper awareness of your anger or joy—again, later, after the moment—by asking yourself, "What is the thing that I value or need? What is my attachment that is at play here?"

To know why you are experiencing a particular emotion is key to receiving it as the important message your body, mind, and spirit are sending you. If I examine that pizza night gone awry, I can see that my anger was rooted in something I valued: a fun evening for my kids because I love them, and they had worked hard for it. Had I been able to get to that thought in the moment, I would have begun to utilize my higher brain function. I might have discovered my empathy for this poor man, forced to work alone in a restaurant full of screaming kids and a costumed mouse. I might have said, "I'm really sorry. That's a lot for any-one to handle. We will just head to the arcade and eat when we are done."

Awareness leads you to the ability to control what you do next. Controlling emotions is about maintaining your ability to think about and choose how to respond. A person controlled by their emotions might be effusively loving at times and might also become vicious and attack. Awareness creates just enough of a buffer for you to consider your words and actions first. Regulating your emotions does not mean denying them. It means harnessing them.

Think of your emotions like a mustang: beautiful but also wild and potentially dangerous. Once they are harnessed, then they are among the most useful of animals. And perhaps even more than that, horses—and emotions!—make wonderful companions. Once we learn to regulate our emotions, they become useful and wonderful companions. Emotional regulation gives you a choice. You may choose to say something or nothing. You may change the subject. You can choose a loving, compassionate response.

A healthy emotional life requires the expression of your emotions. When we do not express our emotions, whether they be positive or negative, they become harmful to ourselves and to our relationships. An emotion like anger can turn into bitterness or resentment, which will sour any relationship. When you express your anger within a loving relationship, you find relief. You might also choose to forgive, to let it go. In either case, anger can propel you to a purposeful way of addressing the issue at hand.

SELF-DIFFERENTIATION IS THE KEY

We tend to share the emotions of the people and groups to which we are most attached. When I was a child, my parents were upset about the person who was elected president. Their candidate lost. Without even understanding why, I disliked the new president. I took on my parents' dislike for him and the disappointment of losing. I was angry, and I didn't even know why! Today, I look at that president differently. I see the good he did as well. That's because I have differentiated myself from my parents. I respect their views and share many of them, but I came to my own conclusions with my own discernment.

Feelings, thoughts, and ways of doing things get passed on from generation to generation. Tradition can be a good thing—except when it's not. Alcoholism, spousal abuse, out-of-control emotions, or underexpressed emotions are not so good. Unless you want to repeat the harmful cycles of your family or any other group that influences you, then you need to self-differentiate.

Self-differentiation is the ability to distinguish your thoughts and feelings from the thoughts and feelings of others. It is the awareness of the boundary of where you end and another person begins. A lack of self-differentiation leaves you undefined as an individual. Without it, you become only a product of your environment. You think, feel, and act like the people around you. You are largely a representation of them.

In terms of regulating emotions, a lack of self-differentiation means you are being influenced by emotions that aren't even yours. Imagine trying to teach a kindergarten class with one hundred children. How would you maintain control of that class enough to teach? The answer is not to work harder; it is to find other people to teach seventy-five of those children. That class size is simply more than anyone can handle.

Similarly, you are only equipped to manage your own emotions. Your own "class" of emotions is quite enough. Taking on the emotions of others is not sustainable; it's more than anyone can handle. Jesus told us that we will each have our own cross to bear (Luke 9:23). He did not tell us to carry the crosses of others. We do, though. We carry the emotional baggage of the groups and individuals with whom we identify.

By learning to differentiate yourself from others, you will unload many emotional burdens. Self-differentiation is a bit like redemption; it is the freeing of self from bondage to others. In an ideal childhood, children are encouraged to think for themselves and express their emotions. They are encouraged to make well-thought-out choices and follow their own path. Yet we all grow up with some level of needing to please our family by conforming to it. We are all very much products of our families. Self-differentiation gives us the freedom to make different choices.

Often unknowingly, we carry the feelings of our families. We also carry the feelings of our communities, schools, regions, churches, political parties, heroes, and any number of people and groups we rely on and admire. We adopt their values and feelings about things. When the group is unhappy, we are unhappy. When they are happy, we are happy. When our team loses, we feel the loss. When some other group attacks ours, we feel threatened and treat them as our enemy. The things we attach our lives to shape our thoughts, feelings, and behavior.

I am not saying that this is all bad. Belonging to a group involves a certain amount of feeling what the group feels. But we are not free to think, feel, and act differently until we begin to recognize ourselves as unique individuals with the freedom to choose.

Consider your most significant relationships—the people with whom you share your life. If you are undifferentiated from them, your emotions will greatly be shaped by theirs. If you have been in a relationship with an emotionally volatile person, you know that it is like being on a roller coaster—exciting but also nauseating. It isn't your roller coaster that you are on; it is theirs. Self-differentiation means getting off other people's roller coasters.

Again, we naturally attach our lives to others, and that means feeling alongside our loved ones and the groups to which we belong. But it is important to realize that they are not us and we are not them. We must not just be passengers in other people's lives. If you do not learn to differentiate your life from others, then you will not be free to live the life for which God created you.

The apostle Paul wrote, "Do not be conformed to this world, but be transformed by the renewing of your minds, so that you may discern what is the will of God—what is good and acceptable and perfect" (Rom 12:2). We grow up naturally conforming to the world we are raised in and the people who raise us. We conform to our families, our communities, our peers, our idols—the people we want to accept us. Conformity is a mechanism by which our species has evolved to survive. To think, feel, and act differently puts us in danger of being rejected by people and institutions on which we rely.

To learn to live in God's world will take a transformation of the mind. We must shift our highest attachment from things or people to God. Belonging to God not only gives us the sense of security we need to function but also transforms our minds—the way we think, feel, and behave.

But allowing ourselves to be formed by God is different than conforming to the ways of others as we did before. We don't have to do anything in order to be loved and accepted by God. Knowing this frees you to become you—the you that God had in mind from the beginning. Paul tells us that our minds will be given the ability to discern what God's will is—what is good, acceptable, and perfect. Making God your highest attachment begins to restore your brain's ability to discern. When we live in loving relationship with God, the image of God in us is being restored to the original blueprint. Attachment to God and self-differentiation from the world clear the way to our most loving self. And emotional regulation is a key component of self-differentiation.

Let's now look at emotional regulation from a brain science perspective.

YOUR THREE BRAINS

Emotional regulation is a function of your prefrontal cortex. It is the brain matter directly behind your forehead. The prefrontal cortex is part of the brain generally called the neocortex. From an evolutionary perspective, it is the newest (*neo*) development of the brain. Humans share this with other animals, to varying degrees. Your neocortex gives you the ability to think, talk, discern, reason, empathize, self-differentiate, and perform any number of higher cognitive functions. One might make the case that our neocortex is the part of us that most reflects the image of God.

In a sense, humans have not one brain but three. The neocortex is the newest of the three brains. The oldest part of your brain is the brain stem, which we share with all vertebrates. It is in the back of your brain connecting the rest of your nervous system to your brain. Your brain stem has one sole purpose: survival. It regulates your basic survival functions like breathing and heartbeat. We don't have to think at all to breathe; the brain stem takes care of it. It also utilizes your senses to scan for danger. Some have referred to the brain stem as the reptilian brain: no emotions or thinking, just survival. All data coming from our senses goes to the brain stem first for a safety check. If you were surrounded by wild animals all the time, you would need this instinct to survive. However, if you allow your brain stem to rule your life, you will be quite a dangerous animal—especially when you're feeling threatened.

The middle part of your brain is referred to as the limbic system. The limbic system houses your emotions and memories. Data from the brain stem arouses emotion and engages with memory in order to prepare your body to respond to potential threats in the environment. In minimalist terms, think of your emotions as a signal for what's good or bad, what is wanted, and what is to be feared. The basic purpose of memory is to help determine, based on historical data, what is good for us and what is dangerous. If you were once bitten by a snake, then your limbic system will remind you that snakes are bad, even if not all snakes are dangerous. Anytime you see or feel anything that resembles a

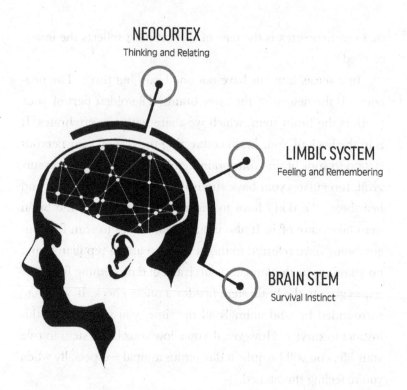

NEOCORTEX
Thinking and Relating

LIMBIC SYSTEM
Feeling and Remembering

BRAIN STEM
Survival Instinct

snake, your limbic system pulls the fire alarm and prepares your body for fight, flight, or freeze.

So your neocortex—the most recently evolved part of the human brain—gives you the ability to *interpret* what you are experiencing and to respond reasonably. It can help you to examine the snakelike thing on your walking path more carefully and see that, in fact, it is a stick.

The problem is that the information gathered by your senses reaches the neocortex last. This means that unless you find a way to slow or stop the processes that began in your reptilian brain stem and moved to your limbic system, then your actions will be governed by emotion. You will act out of fear or appetite. You will see good, and you will eat. You will see bad, and you will fight, run, or freeze. No thinking in between. Emotion, if unchecked, is mindlessness.

So we could say that the neocortex holds the key to loving relationship. When we stay in relational mode, we interrupt our animal instincts to fight, flight, and freeze. We consider the other, not just our own survival, in our choices for response.

HOW HEALTHY ATTACHMENT REGULATES YOUR EMOTIONS

Our brains are wired for attachment. We rely on our attachments for emotional well-being. Your limbic system, which houses your emotions in the brain, is impacted by the environment, including people. Your emotions influence other people's emotions, and their emotions influence yours. When you develop an attachment to a person, then an exchange of emotion goes on. Think about a baby and a mother again. The mother has a huge impact on the baby's emotional state. Moms have the ability to regulate their babies' emotions. They can even help regulate their heartbeat. When we respond to a crying child with love and concern and a calming manner, if the child has a secure attachment to us, then the child will be comforted . . . eventually. All parents know it can take some time—and may also require food and a diaper change. But a resonance develops between child and caretaker, one that allows for regulation and even revision of emotion. A mother's smile can turn a mood in a heartbeat.

This continues into adulthood in a number of ways. Other people are part of my emotional regulation system. My wife is a great comfort to me. We have emotional resonance with each other through our attachment to each other. I can comfort her, and she can comfort me. I still call my parents sometimes when I am upset. I rely on other people, too, like my therapist, my doctor, and my close friends. If any of these people lack self-differentiation, then they would only be able to suffer with me rather than also calm my fears. But because they are self-differentiated, they are able to be calm when I am not.

No human being can or should carry your emotional load and take responsibility for your care. If you over-rely on others emotionally, you move into what is called codependency. Codependency keeps us emotionally stunted and leads to unhealthy relationship patterns. It can even open us up to abuse. Codependency gives another person control of your life.

The answer to this dilemma, given by many, is that you must learn to be self-reliant. Self-reliance is a very highly valued characteristic in American culture. It means that you take responsibility for your life. Many of us like the idea of self-reliance because it means we don't have to help other people—or ask for help ourselves. But self-reliance ultimately goes against both our evolutionary nature and our God-created nature. We evolved to need each other, and God created us to need each other. Our reliance on others is inescapable and quite within God's intention for us. It's important not to confuse self-differentiation with self-reliance.

God can become your primary emotional regulator, along with the supporting cast of people in your life. God will be like a mother, soothing your fears and restoring your mind to clearer discernment and more loving engagement.

JESUS AND EMOTIONAL REGULATION

Jesus is the model for what a secure attachment with God looks like. He is God's son and enjoys perfect security, knowing nothing in this world can change that fact. He has been, is, and will be God's own child. You are too.

Perhaps one of Jesus's most difficult days was the day he learned that his cousin John the Baptist was unjustly and unceremoniously executed. When John's disciples tell Jesus about his cousin's death, Matthew writes that Jesus withdrew by himself to a deserted place in a boat. Presumably, Jesus went away to deal with the variety of emotions he was experiencing, as well as to connect with the source of his comfort and peace, God. In their book *Burnout: The Secret to Unlocking the Stress Cycle*, the authors ask the question, "Does suffering alone build character?" Their answer: "No. These things leave you more vulnerable to further injury. What makes you stronger is whatever happens to you *after* you survive the thing that didn't kill you. What makes you stronger is *rest*."

I cannot read this passage without remembering one of my own worst days. A voice from the intercom summoned my brother and me to the school office. Our parents were picking us up to go home. It was quiet in the car on the way to our house. They wanted to wait to tell us the bad news until we were home. Our cousin, who was about the same age as us, had been killed by a car on his way to school that morning.

"Before we leave to join the rest of our family in San Antonio, I want you to go find a place to be by yourselves," our mother said after they had broken the news. "You can think and feel and do whatever you want. You can talk to God or just be quiet." It was the quiet before the storm of emotion we would all experience.

We are not told if Jesus prayed or how long he was by himself after his cousin was killed, but it was enough time for him to get what he needed for what was to come. Swarms of grieving and anxious people were looking for him. John was their prophet, their leader, and now he was dead. Now they would begin to look to Jesus.

When crisis or tragedy hits us, or when people need us, our instincts may tell us to stay in the boat and keep paddling. But Jesus did something quite different. When he saw the great crowd like sheep without a shepherd, his grief turned to compassion. The difference between grief and compassion is the prefix com-, which means "with." Jesus suffered with these people. He was not alone in his grief. However, his grief didn't shut down his ability to function lovingly. Rather than withdrawing further, he began to cure their sick. Perhaps he couldn't bring his cousin back, but he could do something to alleviate the suffering of those who loved John. It was an outpouring of love.

Emotional regulation is about experiencing the full breadth of the emotions of the human experience and turning it all into loving action. Emotions do not have to be the things that trip us up in relationships; they can be the fuel for our love. The key is connecting with the Source of all love.

REFLECTION QUESTIONS

1. When have you felt like your emotions overrode your ability to think? In other words, when did you let your lizard brain take over?

2. What do you do to process your emotions when you have had a bad day?

3. What do you need to do for yourself to maintain a loving mindset toward others?

4. What emotions have you experienced lately, and which attachments do they point to?

SPIRITUAL INTELLIGENCE EXERCISES: EXTRACTING NEEDS FROM EMOTION AND CELEBRATING THE SABBATH

These two short exercises can help us learn to differentiate our emotions from those of others. Naming the needs at the center of our emotions can help us sort through where our emotions come from. And celebrating the Sabbath—resting—can give us the space and pause necessary to get distance from our emotions and figure out which are truly ours and which aren't.

Extracting Needs from Emotions

1. Identify an emotion that you are experiencing.

2. If it is positive, ask yourself, "What need is being met?"

3. If it is negative, ask, "What need is *not* being met?"

The awareness you will gain from these questions will provide a way to identify what needs are being met and how, as well as what needs are not being met. Satisfying your basic emotional needs will put you in a better position to attend to the needs of others.

Celebrate the Sabbath

1. Get all your chores and meals prepared before your Sabbath begins.

2. Begin at sundown either Friday evening or Saturday evening; continue through sundown the next day. Find a way to mark the beginning of the Sabbath; you could light a candle, turn off your phone, say a prayer, sing a song, jump for joy.

3. Only do things that nourish and rest your mind, body, and spirit. Try to do nothing out of obligation. Sleep in, play games, eat your favorite meal with your favorite people, nap, enjoy nature, pray, create art, listen to music, dance, whatever you might be called to do. Be mindful of God in everything, giving thanks along the way.

4. As sundown approaches, give thanks to God for everything good about the day. Consider making this your weekly practice.

Practicing Sabbath will create space and time for meeting some of your basic needs as well as attending to relationships that matter to you. It will also help you to learn to trust that even when you stop working, God will still take care of you.

PRAYER

O Creator of emotion, I confess that I have let my emotions control me. All too often I have allowed fear, shame, and anger to keep me from loving as you created me to love. Help me to maintain a loving state of mind. There is not a moment that you do not love me and seek to show your love to me. Help me to remain open to your love, that I may love others.

God, right now I need _____.

Lead me, Lord, in discerning your will as I respond to others in need or who threaten me. Amen.

6 | THE PATH OF VULNERABILITY

It takes a lot of energy to not be you.

Many of us spend a lot of energy trying to cover up the parts of us we believe will be unacceptable to other people and projecting the image of who we think others want us to be. Only when we are loved and accepted, just as we are, can we let go of the need to be someone else. Having the security to be vulnerable saves your energy for loving relationships and pursuits that give you fulfillment and enjoyment.

And the real you isn't just someone you grow into; it's someone that you have always been. The problem many of us have is that we have left that person behind at some stage of our lives.

I will never forget the question a therapist once asked me: "Paul, when was it that you began to cover up who you are?" As I reflected on that question, I realized it wasn't that I had lost who I am; it is that I began to hide the parts of me that I was insecure about.

There were probably instances of this cover up long before I entered the sixth grade. But that was the year when two clear desires emerged in me: (1) the desire to not be made fun of by my classmates and (2) the desire to be accepted by them.

A girl I liked had said to me in the hallway, "Your breath stinks, Paul." It embarrassed me, and it made me feel self-conscious. It caused me to pull back when I talked to people and made me a little standoffish. It also made me afraid to talk to girls I liked.

It seems like such a small thing, right? But shame is never a small thing. "Shame is the intensely painful feeling or experience of believing that we are flawed and therefore unworthy of love and belonging," writes vulnerability and shame researcher Brené Brown. Shame is a huge disrupter of spiritual intelligence. I didn't know exactly what it took to be accepted by sixth graders, but I was learning what was *unacceptable*.

I am fortunate to have had parents who loved me as I am. I didn't experience much shame at home. Guilt, yes, but shame, no. But we live in a world of shamed people. And shamed people shame people. Shame makes its way into all of us sooner or later. It makes us believe that we cannot be loved as we are. It makes us cover up our true selves, which we or others have deemed unlovable. Our response is to try to conform to the people we want to love us.

The irony is that your true self won't ever receive love that way. People may love the *persona* you portray. But when shame fuels your life, your truest self will be love-starved. The path to your true and most loving self includes learning to be vulnerable.

So self-differentiation is about becoming free from the control of others or the need to control others. Forgiveness helps us self-differentiate by freeing us from the control of resentment, and emotional regulation frees us from the tyranny of acting impulsively on our own or others' emotions. Vulnerability is the freedom to be ourselves as we are right now, wounds and all.

THE PATH FORWARD BEGINS BY GOING BACK

The path of vulnerability begins with going back. Somewhere in your past is a child who was free and vulnerable. That child had no shame yet. That child laughed, played, said whatever was on their mind, and experienced their emotions fully without hiding. And they received and expressed love without worry.

We weren't complete and mature people when we were kids. We weren't responsible for much of anything. We threw temper tantrums. We hit our siblings. But we knew how to receive and share love without fear. That's what we have to get back to in order to move forward.

Jesus's disciples argued about who was the greatest among them. That's a very ego-driven argument. When we feel insecure about something, we have a need to overcompensate. I can't speak for women, but most men I know have a desire to be great. We want to be the fastest kid at recess. We want to be the best at math. We enter a career path and want to conquer our industry. Underneath all this bravado, however, is a need to be loved, but all too often we don't feel it is acceptable to ask for it. When the disciples came to Jesus and asked, "Who is the greatest in the kingdom of heaven?" I wonder if they were really asking, "Who do you love the most?"

We have all had moments of feeling less than lovable. In order to not be hurt again, we harden the outer wall of our hearts, and we want to be invulnerable. The Latin root of the word *vulnerable* is *vulner,* which means "wound." To be vulnerable, then, is to be woundable. Many of our wounds receive the attention they need, but some wounds remain unhealed. They get paved over and are hard to access. In those wounds is a child who is lost and needs to be found and loved.

Up until around age eight, my son would ask me at bedtime, "Dad, will you snuggle with me?" We would lie there quietly or chat about what was going on in his inquisitive mind. At some point, he would say for no reason, "Dad, I love you." Then he would turn his head and fall asleep.

This is how Jesus responded to the disciples' bravado: "He called a child, whom he put among them, and said, 'Truly I tell you, unless you change and become like children, you will never enter the kingdom of heaven. Whoever becomes humble like this child is the greatest in the kingdom of heaven. Whoever welcomes one such child in my name welcomes me'" (Matt 18:2–5). Jesus saw through the bravado of these grown men. He saw insecure little boys who needed to be loved. I imagine he took this little child—perhaps one of the disciples' children—and put his arms around the child as he said the words. Perhaps they thought the kingdom of heaven was something to be understood like a math problem. But in fact, the kingdom is allowing yourself to be lovingly embraced by God, like a parent enfolds their child with love. I wonder if Jesus was trying to help those men remember when they were vulnerable little boys who just wanted to be hugged and told they were loved.

There is a child in you who is waiting to be welcomed and embraced. You have to go back and tend to that child before you can move forward. That child, who was not afraid to ask and even cry for help, needs voice in your life.

Can you identify times when you were embarrassed, ashamed, or rejected when you were young? When you felt less than lovable or acceptable? What would you say to such a child? You'd probably put your arms around them and tell them that you love them. You'd probably do whatever you could to make them feel safe, loved, and accepted.

GETTING WHAT WE NEED

At some point in your life, whether you were a child or an adult, whether you were raised in a healthy, loving environment or an unhealthy, unloving one, you didn't get what you needed. Insecurity begins when our needs aren't being met, particularly when we are young. Think of cement that has not fully dried. You can very easily make an impression on the wet cement with your hands or feet. Once the concrete is dried, those impressions are permanent. It will also take quite a bit of force to make new impressions on hardened cement. When we are young, it doesn't take much to make a lasting impression. The impressions made on us when we are young are lasting, for better or for worse. The way to repair those early impressions is to fill them in with fresh cement.

No, you can't go back in time and undo things in your childhood. But if you can identify the places in you that need filling, you can fill them now by getting what you need now. Aren't we always trying to fill these places in one way or another?

In an earlier chapter, we identified two very basic first beliefs that shape our whole relational lives. They are the answers to two questions:

1. Am I worthy of love?
2. Can I trust others to love me?

If you can wholeheartedly say yes to these questions, then you are most likely a secure person. These questions were answered for you as a little child by the way your parents responded to your needs. It means they lovingly and reliably responded to you very consistently. The times that you did not get this from your caregivers left gaps in your ability to believe you are loved and believe that others can be trusted.

So how do you fill the gaps as an adult? As Jesus said, we must become like children again. That is, we must embrace vulnerability. This doesn't mean you should be vulnerable with everyone, in every situation, all the time. Think of this as having a procedure done by a medical professional; that is, you wouldn't just let anyone operate on you. Being vulnerable as an adult will require trusting your hidden and wounded self with another. It will require experiencing your shame and your fear.

"To relationally confront our shame requires that we risk feeling it on the way to its healing," writes psychiatrist Curt Thompson. He continues, "This is no easy task. This is the common undercurrent of virtually all of our relational brokenness.

We sense, imagine, feel, and think all sorts of things that we never say because we're far too frightened to be that honest, that vulnerable. But honest vulnerability is the key to both healing shame—and its inevitably anticipated hellish outcome of abandonment—and preventing it from taking further root in our relationships and culture."

Shame cannot be healed in a vacuum. It requires bringing the hidden parts of ourselves into view of another person. Shame was created relationally, and it is healed relationally. When we speak of the things that make us feel shame to a person who listens without judgment and with compassion, our shame gets released. Our shame is replaced by affirmation.

Allowing yourself to be seen and known by people who support and love you will build your confidence and courage to be you all the time. It may start with one person you feel safe with. It could be a therapist, a pastor, a friend, or your spouse. It might even be a stranger on an airplane.

When I first started having panic attacks and anxiety, I found it hard to understand what was going on. I also found it hard to talk about my experiences. One time during that season, I was on a flight back from a preaching conference. All week, as a leader at the conference, I had been experiencing panic. Now the plane was packed, and I was squeezed into the window seat. I felt trapped. The weather was bad, and we experienced a lot of turbulence during the flight.

The man next to me was a big, jovial fellow and seemed open to talking. I decided to take a leap of faith and tell him what I was experiencing. It was clear that he cared about what I was going through. I said, "Can you please just keep talking to me? It helps."

So for two hours, this dear man told me funny stories about his life. I felt like a scared little boy being read a bedtime story by my dad. Those interactions kept me from hyperventilating, and his care lifted my spirit. I can't imagine the hell I would have experienced if I had suffered alone.

Shame and fear want to isolate you. Leaning into vulnerable relationships is the path forward. Start by telling someone what you need.

THREE MODES OF INSECURITY

We all experience some level of insecurity, and our insecurity shows up in different modes. If we can learn to recognize that we are acting out of fear, it will help us to address it. Our fears are obstacles to being vulnerable, which is the only way to experience and share love—with God and with others. Many people just mindlessly live out their insecurities and then wonder why they cannot experience deep, meaningful connection with others.

We don't always act out of our insecurity. But when faced with a threat or a crisis, the hurt child in us will act out. We can go from a mature adult to a cranky toddler or a surly teenager in a heartbeat. We can shut down and withdraw to our rooms. We might be like a kid who comes home from school, and when Dad asks how they are, they say, "Fine"—when in fact they are not.

Becoming aware of when you are feeling insecure is essential to learning to be vulnerable. There are three basic ways our insecurity shows up: pretending, defending, and offending.

We pretend when we believe that others will not accept us as we are. We cover up the parts of ourselves that we think people would reject, and we project the person we believe people want to see. We pretend to be someone we are not. God gives you everything you need to be who you are intended to be. However, God does not give you what you need to be someone else. That is what exhausts and frustrates us. You must learn to trust that being you is enough.

Underneath all the insecurity of pretending, every person is beautiful, lovable, and endlessly fascinating. But our various

THREE MODES OF INSECURITY

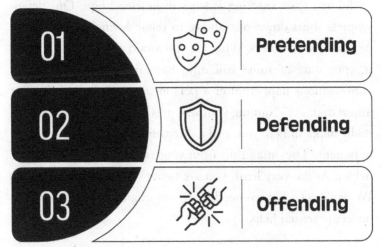

01 🎭 **Pretending**

02 🛡 **Defending**

03 👊 **Offending**

insecurities—most of which come from feeling unloved and wounded—create someone we are not. Hateful people are not truly hateful. Their fears have taken over their lives and their character. Boring people are not really boring. They have just learned to hide the fascinating-ness of their lives because some idiot made them feel uninteresting.

A second mode of insecurity is defending. When we are covering up a wound, shame, or fear, we are prone to defensiveness. We are either afraid of being discovered as frauds, or we are protecting a wound. We are afraid of rejection or reinjury, and so we begin to defend ourselves. Defensiveness comes out of our basic survival instincts. If you feel yourself getting defensive, ask yourself: What am I protecting?

Sometimes defending oneself or other people is quite necessary. Our defensive instincts developed in the wild, where predators may attack at any time. Those instincts are not as useful in a team meeting at work or in friendships. Our defensiveness shuts down our ability to relate lovingly or even just rationally with others. What are you afraid of? If you can name it, your state of mind will shift. Sometimes the most helpful conversations happen after a person says, "I'm sorry. I'm just afraid that. . . ." Naming your fear gets you in touch with what's really happening in you, and it often elicits the empathy of your opponent. They may shift from your perceived enemy to your helper. At the very least, you are being vulnerable and honest. We can't get what we need if we are in a defensive mode. We deflect potential help.

Certainly, there are human predators as well. But ask yourself if your life is in danger right now. Pause before you end up moving into the third mode of insecurity: offending.

Once insecurity has taken over our ability to control ourselves, we sometimes go on the attack. It may just be a biting insult or passive-aggressive behavior, but insecurity can lead us to hurt others. Hurt people hurt people if they do not get the healing they need. We may even be oblivious that we are doing to others the thing that was done to us. Usually, the person we are attacking isn't the person we *think* we are attacking. They may just remind you of someone who hurt you. Perhaps they are just a safer target for your pain.

Pretending, defending, and offending are all symptoms of the same problem, and they have the same solution: being vulnerable enough with someone to get the love, the forgiveness, the healing, the affirmation you need.

I have struggled with defensiveness. Just ask any boss who has given me a performance review. It happens in my marriage as well. I don't take criticism well. It occurred to me one day that I get defensive and sometimes even offensive when I feel underappreciated. The best thing I ever did for my marriage was tell my wife that I needed appreciation. She does it wonderfully and authentically. I feel silly that I need this, and that's probably why I struggled to voice it. When I cook for the family, she tells me how much she appreciates the way I show love. When I am about to leave the house for a speaking engagement, she tells me how well I will do and how sharp I look. They're little things, but she gives them to me because she loves me, and she knows I need them.

Being vulnerable helps you get what you need to be secure, but it doesn't stop there.

YOUR VULNERABILITY IS FOR THE SAKE OF OTHERS

God did not put us on this earth just to get what we need. God helps us get what we need so that others can get what they need. When we receive love, we are better able to love others. When we receive healing, we are better able to help others receive healing.

Vulnerability is a bit like the damper on my barbecue smoker. If I keep the damper closed, the fire dies, and I can't serve amazing food to the ones I love. When the damper is open, then oxygen gets in and fuels the fire, which creates the heat and smoke necessary to turn raw meat into smoked goodness. Without the ability to be vulnerable, no love gets in, and no love gets out. No healing gets in, and no healing gets out. Certainly, there are times when the damper needs to be partially closed, or the fire can get too hot. Being vulnerable is something we must learn to discern when to be.

All that we receive from God is intended to go beyond meeting our own needs. When we have gotten the resources we need, we are in a better position to share with others. I must note here that people with practically nothing to share are often the most generous people. We have to widen our definition of resources to include intangible ones. Sharing sacrificially is at the heart of the life of Christ. The Hebrew prophet Isaiah wrote of the future savior, "By his wounds we are healed" (Isa 53:5). Henri Nouwen, in *The Wounded Healer*, writes, "Nobody escapes being wounded. We all are wounded people, whether physically, emotionally, mentally, or spiritually. The main question is not 'How can we hide our wounds?' so we don't have to be embarrassed. The question is, 'How can we put our woundedness in the service of others?' When our wounds cease to be a source of shame and become a source of healing, we have become wounded healers."

People don't need your wisdom nearly as much as they need to know they are not alone and that there is hope for healing. When we offer ourselves as we truly are, wounds and all, we give a great and powerful gift for the sake of others.

A man about my age came to see me at the church office. His parents had recommended talking with me. He was racked with anxiety. As he described his experience, I could relate to everything as I knew just how paralyzing anxiety can be. I knew how hard it must have been for him to just to leave his house and ask a stranger for help. At the same time, my self-differentiated mindset reminded me that I was not him and that I was not feeling what he was feeling. I could have easily been dragged into his anxiety. I had to fight that impulse. So instead, I shared some coping skills for anxiety. I led him through some breathing exercises. I advised him to seek professional help and referred him to a therapist. I also shared a bit about my own experience with anxiety. I told him that after a lot of work and help, I was able to manage my anxiety and even experience healing, and I was confident that he would too.

The next Sunday, his mother approached me and thanked me for meeting with her son. "The thing that helped him the most and convinced him to seek help was that you had been through it too," she said. "He saw hope for himself in your struggle."

Our vulnerability—our woundedness—can produce one of the most powerful healing agents in existence: empathy.

REFLECTION QUESTIONS

1. When was it that you first covered up who you are—and why?

2. If you could go back in time and speak to yourself at a time when you felt most afraid to be you, what would you say?

3. When are you able to be at your most vulnerable?

4. How does being open and honest about ourselves, including our sin and shame, help both ourselves and other people?

SPIRITUAL INTELLIGENCE PRACTICE: OLD SELF VERSUS NEW SELF

We are all in the process of letting go of our old survival-based selves. And what do we replace that self with? The apostle Paul wrote, "So if anyone is in Christ, there is a new creation: everything old has passed away; see, everything has become new!" (2 Cor 5:17). As we move out of our survival selves, we can embrace our "new creation" selves—selves that are both loved and loving.

This exercise will help you to self-differentiate from your old self and embrace who you are becoming in Christ.

1. Make a big T on a piece of paper. At the top of the T, write the name of a person, experience, group, or cultural factor that has shaped you, for better or worse.

2. On the left side of the T, write, "Who I am in _____." Describe who you are in that space. For example, Who I am in the presence of my father. In the presence of my mother-in-law. As an employee. As a victim of violence.

3. On the right side of the T, write, "Who I am in Christ." Describe who you are as a follower of Christ or a child of God.

4. Look at who you are, all of it—the good, the bad, and the ugly. Know that God deeply loves that person. Look with loving eyes at that person. Forgive that person. Thank that person. Let go of that person.

5. If you wrote the name of a person at the top of your T, do the same for that person. Know that God deeply loves that person. Look with loving eyes on that person. Forgive that person, if you can. Thank that person, if you can. Let go of that person, if you can.

6. Then look at who you are becoming as you look to move toward the right side of the T, your Christlike side. Welcome this new creation. And whenever your old self shows up, continue to love them, forgive them, thank them, and let them go.

PRAYER

O Lord, for my sake you made yourself vulnerable by being born as a baby just like me. For my sake you exposed yourself to rejection, injustice, and even death. Give me the courage to be vulnerable, that I may receive greater healing and for the sake of loving others. Help me to become vulnerable enough to receive healing by receiving you into the painful and shamed parts of my life.

O God, give me the courage to be honest about _____.

Through my vulnerability and by your grace, shame is on the way out of my life, and healing is on the way in. Amen.

Part III

EMPATHY: BECOMING A CONDUIT OF GOD'S LOVE FOR OTHERS

7 | THE PATH OF LISTENING TO OTHERS

Becoming spiritually intelligent is about receiving God's love, but it is also about being a source of God's love for others. Once we are securely attached to God—the source of love—and once we are self-differentiated from a world focused on survival, we are in a much better position to share God's love with others. Now we can rest securely in God's love, trusting that God will be with us. Now we are no longer controlled by our environment or our emotions or others, and we have no need to control these things either. We are free to love the world as God does.

Babies cannot survive without the loving care of a parental figure. As adults, we may be able to survive, but we will never thrive without loving connections to other people. The connective tissue between people is called *empathy*. Empathy—the capacity to feel what another person is feeling—connects us with each other and opens the way for loving, life-giving relationships.

Part of becoming your most loving self is recognizing that you are different from other people and that other people are different from you. That's self-differentiation, as we discussed in detail in the chapters in part II. If you are unable to self-differentiate, then you will project the way you feel on other people, or you will lose your sense of self in the feelings of others. Empathy helps you to connect with people even though they are different from you. The goal of spiritual intelligence is to be able to receive and share God's love. Empathy, then, can be a pathway of God's love through us. The goal of empathy is to understand what another person is experiencing so that we can meet them in their point of need. Empathy is fundamental to loving, life-giving relationships. Empathy can change the course of a person's day or even their life.

Air travel often makes me anxious, especially when I am on my way to some important function in which I have a role. I hate to be late, and with air travel, lots of factors are completely out of my control. It had been one of those days. Everything had gotten delayed, and I was going to have to rent a car for the last leg of the journey in order to make it to my conference in time. I had already been surly to the airline booking agent, and now I was headed for the rental car agency. I was full of pent-up anger, looking for a target. You know me well enough by now to know what might happen next, right?

The young woman behind the counter at the rental car agency must have recognized the look on my face as I approached. She'd probably seen it a thousand times. Rather than bracing for my fury, however, she softened her expression. "You look like you've had a difficult day," she said with genuine concern. "I'm going to do everything I can to make it better."

Anger is rarely a true emotion. It is usually a more acceptable feeling that covers up fear—an emotion that makes us feel vulnerable. My anger quickly dissipated because of the empathy that young woman showed me. She saw my fear of being late, and she addressed that fear rather than my anger. Her kindness and optimism changed everything. I had tears in my eyes as I thanked her.

The world needs a lot more empathy. People need to be seen and heard and felt and understood. The three paths of empathy that we will explore are listening to others, feeling what others are feeling, and responding with loving action. We can see all three of these pathways in that brief but powerful interaction I just described with the rental car agent. Without empathy, God's love will always be blocked.

LISTENING: THE SHORTEST PATH TO UNDERSTANDING ANOTHER

Some people—sometimes called empaths—intuitively recognize the feelings of others. They feel those feelings without even trying. Others struggle to identify the feelings of others and respond to people obliviously, not recognizing what they are going through in a given moment. We will address this aspect of empathy—feeling with another—in the next chapter.

If the goal of empathy is understanding another person's experience and meeting them where they are, then there is an efficient path that anybody can learn: listening. We do not have to intuit or guess what people are experiencing; we can ask them. I am glad that the young woman at the rental car desk recognized my feelings before she spoke. But even if she hadn't had that skill, she could have simply said, "How are you doing today?

I know air travel can be challenging." Just asking and then listening gets you most of the way toward what naturally empathetic people do.

"How are you doing?" may be a question you ask or hear a lot. But how many people pause long enough to actually give others a chance to respond? A colleague of mine modifies the question. "How are you *really* doing today?" he'll say and then wait as if he has all the time in the world. Not everyone takes him up on the offer, but we always appreciate it.

Listening to others shows them that they matter. Children's television icon Fred Rogers said in an interview, "Listening is where love begins." When we listen, we show we care. Listening opens the way to loving, and people are thirsty for it. "Find someone to listen to you," wrote the poet John Fox. "When someone deeply listens to you, it is like a dented cup you've had since childhood. You watch it fill up with cold, fresh water. And when it balances on top of the brim, you are understood. When it overflows and touches your skin, you are loved." To be listened to well is to be understood and loved. Very few people are really listened to on a regular basis.

JESUS LISTENS EVEN WHILE OTHERS SHUSH

If you were blind and living in the first century, you didn't have many options. You had to rely on help from others, either from family or strangers. Bartimaeus is described in the Gospels as a blind beggar. That was how the world knew him. He would have been a familiar sight, sitting there outside of Jericho. Most likely, no one knew anything about him except that he was blind and that he was a beggar.

As Jesus and company were passing by, Bartimaeus inquired who was passing. When he heard it was Jesus, he began to shout, "Jesus, Son of David, have mercy on me!" (Mark 10:47). Some of the people with Jesus began to shush him. I am sure they just thought he was going to ask Jesus for money. An important man like Jesus can't be bothered by a guy like Bartimaeus. Plus, they had to get to Jerusalem. Let's keep it moving.

But Bartimaeus just yelled louder. He desperately wanted to be heard by Jesus, and everyone else just wanted him to be quiet.

Have you ever been shushed? It is a horrible feeling. It makes you feel like you don't matter. If a person is shushed enough times, they just give up trying, like a baby in an overcrowded orphanage when they finally accept that a caregiver won't be coming. Perhaps Bartimaeus had almost given up, but he had heard about Jesus. Jesus could do much more than toss a few coins his way. And Jesus was merciful. Jesus would listen to him even if everyone else shushed him. So Bartimaeus would cry out until he was heard.

Jesus heard him. He told his disciples, "Call him to me." When they did, he jumped up and ran to Jesus, throwing off his cloak, something valuable and necessary for survival in a cold world. Jesus didn't give him a lecture about taking responsibility for his life. He certainly didn't shush him. He asked him a question: "What do you want me to do for you?"

Bartimaeus must have been dumbfounded for a moment. Who had ever asked him such a question? This is the question a servant asks his master, not what a great teacher asks of a nobody like him. Bartimaeus was bold, though, and he said, "My teacher, let me see again."

Jesus didn't perform any procedures or give him any instructions about how to see. He simply said, "Go; your faith has made you well." Immediately Bartimaeus regained his sight and followed Jesus down the path.

He was healed because he was heard.

KEYS TO EMPATHETIC LISTENING

When we empathetically listen to others, we give them a safe and inviting space to say out loud the things that are keeping them from receiving and sharing God's love: their deep fears, hurts, and resentments. Being heard brings healing to our broken trust system.

So how do we listen in such a way that people feel heard enough to speak the truth about their lives? Here are eight keys to empathetic listening.

Check your ego at the door. A 2013 study from the Max Planck Institute revealed that the main obstacle to our empathy is the projection of our own feelings onto other people.

This projection of our feelings is referred to as emotional egocentricity bias (EEB), which is the tendency to rely too heavily on one's own perspective or have a higher opinion of oneself than reality warrants. The apostle Paul wrote, "Do nothing from selfish ambition or conceit, but in humility regard others as better than yourselves" (Phil 2:3).

I am not saying we are all egomaniacs. But we all live in our own perspectives most of the time. Even our mood, when we are speaking to someone, can impact how we hear people. The 2013 study showed that if a person was in a happy mood, they assumed that everyone else they spoke to must also be happy. Our feelings and perspectives color the way we see and hear others. They can unintentionally shush others. We have to check our egos at the door and allow the other person's perspectives to rise to the top of our perceptions.

Believe that every person is worthy of your ears. We don't mean to do it, but we listen to others better when we feel they are more valuable to us. We listen to our employers because we need them to survive. We listen to people we consider wise. We listen to people who have done things for us. We are naturally on the selfish side, and it shows in our listening.

What if we considered that every person we met was equally valuable? What if you believed that every person has something priceless to offer you? It would change the way you listen. Yes, I know that some people take more than they give to us. But I still want to challenge you to look deeper at the intrinsic value of every human being. Every person ever born is priceless to God. Only God truly knows the true value of every living thing. If you believe that there is gold in every person, you will look for it, and that will change how you listen.

Take time to listen. When your EEB kicks in, the part of your brain that allows you to have empathy for others shuts down. The number one cause of EEB is being in a hurry. To reactivate the empathy part of your brain—just in case you're interested, it's called the right supramarginal gyrus—you must slow down. Just like Jesus stopped for Bartimaeus, to hear people, we must stop for them. I know you have things to do, places to go, and people to see. But what if the person God most wants you to pay attention to is crying out right in front of you?

If it is not possible to listen to someone right now, then when would be a good time? Clear some time off your calendar to listen to them. Don't be in a rush. People can feel your hurry, and it is like a silent shush. They will feel it. You will not be able to hear them in the way they need to be heard if you cannot take the time.

Pay attention to feelings. While it is very important to listen to the words another is speaking, their feelings carry the deeper meaning. We must tap into our ability to feel what other people are feeling to truly understand what is being said. A University of Toronto study on empathy revealed that opportunities to empathize with others occur when one observes the emotions of another person or stranger.

Again, being able to parse out another person's feelings from your own requires self-differentiation: the ability to distinguish your feelings from the feelings of others. You must be aware of your own feelings in the moment as well. This awareness then helps you tap into another person's feelings without losing your sense of self or confusing their feelings with yours.

Realize that transformation comes from their words about their life, not your words. This is a hard thing for most of us to accept. We so often think we know better, and so our tendency is to dispense advice and solutions.

Psychiatrist Curt Thompson writes, "Transformation requires a collaborative interaction, with one person emphatically listening and responding to the other so that the speaker has the experience, perhaps for the first time, of feeling felt by another." Speaking and being heard and felt by another person leads to healing and ultimately transformation.

Listen without judgment and with compassion. Nothing shuts down a person like judgment—and even what may seem, to most people, like mild criticism. Nothing draws a person to share more than empathy.

A pastor of thirty years participated in one of the groups that I led. He was considering retiring. As he thought back over his vocation, he felt that all his effort was wasted. He thought he wasn't making a difference and that nobody cared.

I had asked people to talk about a difficult experience in their childhood. Others had spoken, while he quietly listened. I gently urged him to consider sharing as well. He started talking about his childhood and interrupted himself: "Do you really want to hear this? It seems like every time I try to share something about my past, people tell me to get over it."

One of the others spoke up: "Yes, we care about your experiences!" Every single person in the group nodded, and empathy was written all over their faces. When that pastor was finished sharing, everything about him seemed to change. It was like light was beaming from his face. He had been heard, known, and loved. This experience utterly changed his outlook about ministry. After that meeting, he decided to continue in ministry both with renewed confidence and a clear sense of purpose. Every meeting after that first meeting, his face seemed to glow with lovingness.

When we invite people to speak about their lives, and they discover that they will not be judged, they are freed to be vulnerable. Vulnerability is how we get what we need. Compassion eradicates shame like sunlight does a gloomy day.

Listen like a loving parent listens to a child. The source of our judgment is often that we think that other adults should be able to take care of themselves. After all, they are no longer children; shouldn't they be able to help themselves?

That is simply not true. Humans will always need empathetic ears to be able to heal and grow. To grow in love requires being loved. Love begets love. You simply will not become your most loving self on your own.

Many people are crying out, but we, like toddlers, can't always express ourselves very well. Like the no-longer-blind Bartimaeus, everyone is trying to say, on some level, "Help me!" On the surface, we may just be hearing fussiness or even insults and accusations. But we can know there's a deeper need.

Children sometimes say the most hurtful things they can think of to their parents. In just the last week, I have heard "I hate you" and "I wish I had a different family!" It doesn't feel good to hear this, but as adults, we know that they are children merely asking for love.

What if you listened to adults in the same way? You would be able to hear the deeper needs, and it would open up your empathy more even when they are saying hurtful things to you. Of course, sometimes the appropriate thing to do is to walk away from the conversation. "I will talk with you at some point, when you stop saying hurtful things to me," you could say. Or "We need a break from this conversation, and we can continue it later."

Find someone to listen to you regularly. Think of your ability to listen to others as a cup of water in your spirit. If it is empty, then you have nothing that will support your ability to listen. The only way to fill up your cup is by being listened to by another.

Who are your listeners? A spouse, a friend, a pastor, a counselor, a coach, God? Don't wait until you are empty. Consider being listened to a necessary part of maintaining your well-being and empathy. Set up regular times, whether you think you need them or not. This practice will keep your cup full, not just for yourself but for the sake of others who need your empathetic ears.

Nothing can replace the power of empathetic listening. It's less important what we have to teach others and more important to give others the space to speak the words they need to say. They need to be heard with affirmation and encouragement. To be listened to satisfies a great need: to be loved.

REFLECTION QUESTIONS

1. What is a time in your life when you felt like Bartimaeus: shushed and dismissed?

2. When do you find it hard to listen to people?

3. What are some gifts you received from unlikely people when you took the time to listen to them?

4. Who are the people in your life who listen to you well? How can you make sure you are listened to regularly?

SPIRITUAL INTELLIGENCE EXERCISE: THE LISTENING SCAVENGER HUNT

Learning to recognize others' emotions will activate your empathy and deepen your listening. It can take practice. Listen for the following things in people you encounter this week. You could even check them off as you go. Reflect on how you have learned to identify emotions and what signs you use to identify them.

◆ Happiness

◆ Anger

◆ Worry

◆ Disappointment

◆ Jealousy

◆ Surprise

◆ Excitement

◆ Sadness

◆ Loneliness

◆ Embarrassment

◆ Fear

◆ Curiosity

PRAYER

God, thank you for listening to me in my times of need.
You never shush me when I cry out to you. Open my ears
and hearts for the people you place in my path.

Christ says to me and all people, "What do you want me to do for
you?" God, here is what I want you to do for me. My Teacher, let
me _____.

By faith and through grace, I trust that you will make me
well. I will follow you on the road.

Amen.

8 | THE PATH OF FEELING THE FEELINGS OF OTHERS

Do you feel me? That question generally means, "Do you understand what I am saying?" But it goes deeper than that. *Do you feel me?* evokes the dimension of empathy. Do you feel what I am feeling?

To varying degrees, people have the ability to experience the feelings of others. At its very basic level, empathy is physiological. It is that feeling you have when you see the pain in another person and you feel it.

When people don't feel "felt" by others, it leads to intense feelings of isolation. Being *not* understood, *not* felt, is hellish.

When people are felt by another, great healing and transformation can happen. Being understood by another is like being found. One of the greatest feelings you can experience is that another person gets you. You feel loved.

Part of healthy empathy is feeling what people feel without losing one's sense of well-being or assuming they feel the way you feel. There are actually two ends of the feeling-what-others-are-feeling spectrum. One end means being totally ignorant of other people's feelings. In the previous chapter, I mentioned EEB, in which we project our feelings onto others. EEB can result in you *thinking* you understand another person's feelings, when really it is your ego in disguise. There are also many people who do not strongly feel their feelings and do not naturally recognize feelings in others.

On the other end of the spectrum are people who feel the feelings of others so deeply that they can get overwhelmed by them. They may not be able to tell which feelings belong to whom. Self-differentiation helps us to distinguish our feelings from the feelings of others. It also helps us to have healthy empathy that does not overtax us emotionally.

While we can never fully understand another's experience, sensing the feelings of others gives us helpful clues. Have you ever noticed that when a person comes into the room, the emotion they bring with them can change the feelings of the whole room? You may have been cheerful, and then your coworker comes in, and you sense their anger. Some people seem to carry around an infectious joy, and wherever they go, they leave a residual sense of well-being. Feelings and emotions of others float around in the air like radio waves, and our brains pick them up. We may find ourselves angry or happy and not even know why.

Feeling what other people are feeling is a natural function of empathy. It helps us to understand others. It can also put us at the mercy of the emotional climate in which we live.

WHERE EMPATHY BEGINS: MIRRORING

Have you noticed that when you see someone experience something painful, like bonking their head into a cabinet, you feel it on some level? Have you watched someone eat a delicious dessert and noticed that your mouth was watering? Or seen someone yawn and then yawned yourself? On a very basic, physiological level, you were experiencing empathy. You weren't the one experiencing pain, hunger, or tiredness, but those things triggered something in you that made you feel what another person was experiencing. It's all in your brain.

In 1990, researchers in Italy were observing the brain activity of Macaque monkeys. They attached electronic nodes to the monkeys to monitor their brain activity as they went about their daily routines. One day, as the researchers were taking their lunch break, they noticed that as the monkeys watched them eat, the monkeys' brain activity mirrored the same activity. According to their brain activity, it was as if they were actually eating.

This marked the discovery of mirror neurons, neurons that are activated when we observe other people's experiences. They explain how we can experience fear, joy, or sadness when we watch movies.

Our mirror neurons fire when we observe the feelings of others that we relate to in some way. The deeper the relationship, the more intensely the neurons fire. It began with our first caregiver's face. My mom trained my mirror neurons by her facial expressions and the sound of her voice. She showed me empathy when I cried. Her face mirrored my experience. We first see ourselves in other people. In their faces, our feelings are recognized and hopefully validated. Empathy begins with being empathized with by another person we rely on—an attachment figure.

As we are met with empathetic gestures, those gestures train our minds to recognize feelings and emotions within ourselves and other people. Our mirror neurons are being activated and trained to share experiences with other people. It is important to keep in mind that mirroring begins with our own experiences. Your mirroring system gets activated when another person reflects your experience. This very basic form of empathy is limited to our own experiences.

It's also important to note that other people often experience things that we have very little, if any, grounds to relate to. Our brains work hard to try to make sense of what other people are experiencing, and they will take the closest corresponding experience and use it to try to understand what someone else is experiencing. So, for example, Macaque monkeys know what it is like to be hungry and to eat food. They may not know what a salami sandwich is like, though. Their minds will substitute a sensation of eating some familiar food. We simply cannot perfectly mirror another person's experience. The more we can relate, the stronger our feelings will correspond with another's.

You will never fully understand or know fully what another person is going through. Saying something like "I know *just* what you are going through" is rarely helpful. Yet showing we have some amount of understanding, even if imperfect, can validate another person in their feelings and help them to not feel alone. It will also help build their own empathy system. Empathy begets empathy.

On the other hand, when our distress is met with angry or blank faces and gestures, it confuses our emotional responses. For example, if we learn that our sadness makes other people angry, then two things get put in place. First, we will most likely learn to not express sadness, for fear of an angry response. Second, a mirroring takes place. We may tend to react to another person's sadness with our own anger just like our caregivers did to us. Likewise, if our shame was met with judgment, not only will we hide our shame, but we may judge others in their shame.

In other words, while mirroring can help us learn healthy ways of relating to others, the mirror can also be cracked, giving us a warped view of ourselves and others. Your mirror neurons can be reprogrammed when you are consistently met with empathetic mirroring from others. It will take time and a lot of love from others.

We tend to mirror the people on whom we depend. You could say we are a monkey-see, monkey-do people: we learn through mimicking and mirroring those who cared for us—including the God we believe in.

AN EMPATHETIC GOD

A 2018 study out of the Netherlands explored the impact of religion on human empathy. The researchers found that the religious adherent's view of God had a significant impact on their empathy for others. An empathetic view of God led to empathetic actions and emotions. An unempathetic view of God led to unempathetic actions and emotions.

Think about how you view God. Do you view God as distant, unemotional, uninvolved? Or do you see God as empathetic—able to somehow feel the feelings of humans? Apparently, according to this study, it makes a huge difference.

We won't attempt to examine all the views of God; that would make this book too long. Instead, as we seek to understand Christ-centered spiritual intelligence, we will focus on the God revealed in the Bible and specifically the God represented by Jesus.

When Jesus arrived in Bethany, his close friend Lazarus was already dead and buried. Lazarus's sister Martha met him with both grief and accusation. "Lord, if you had been here, my brother would not have died," she said to Jesus when he finally arrived.

Did Jesus feel her pain? Her anger? Her sadness? Jesus drew close to the tomb where people were weeping, and Lazarus's other sister, Mary, met him and collapsed at his feet in grief. She also said, "Lord, if you had been here, my brother would not have died."

Then the writer of the Gospel of John tells us, "When Jesus saw her weeping, and the Jews who came with her also weeping, he was greatly disturbed in spirit and deeply moved" (John 11:33). If we imagine Jesus's brain at this point in the story, we might safely assume that Jesus's mirror neurons were firing, helping him access the feelings of those around him.

Interestingly enough, the word *disturbed* could also be translated as *angered*. Grief is complicated. Jesus appeared to be picking up *all* the emotions of those around him. Mary's tears moved him deep in his being. They led him to where Lazarus was buried.

And then it happened: Jesus began to weep. His empathy for the mourners literally overflowed. He *felt* them.

We will never know how much of Jesus's weeping was for the sake of the others and how much was for his own grief. Any who experiences empathy knows there is always a degree of mingling of feelings. Reading the story now, we know that Jesus will soon raise Lazarus from the dead. Jesus told the people he would do it. So Jesus knew he would see Lazarus alive in a few minutes. As he did throughout his life, Jesus seemed to live both within the story and outside of it.

And yet he still wept. Many people say that he wept because he was human, and I believe that is true. But perhaps he also wept because God weeps when we weep.

We are created in the image of an empathetic God: a God who cares and a God who feels. When we see and experience God through the person of Jesus, we see God as one who experiences our feelings and even shares them. When the people saw Jesus weep, they exclaimed, "See how he loved him!" When we reflect the feelings of others, we, too, show our love.

In John 8:1–11, we see that Jesus was not controlled by the feelings and emotions of others. A group of male religious authorities had dragged a woman caught in the act of adultery to Jesus in order to test him. Their tradition demanded that a person caught in adultery and witnessed by two or more men—women's testimony did not count—must be stoned to death. Would Jesus uphold their tradition? Would he share their feelings?

Can you feel their judgmental anger? I have no doubt Jesus could feel it. But he chose not to share in it—not to mirror it. He did not respond to their question. Instead, in one of the most fascinating and inscrutable choices we see Jesus make, he bent down and wrote in the dirt.

Perhaps Jesus was just taking a moment to clear himself of their anger or even his own defensiveness, if this is even possible for Jesus. Perhaps he was writing down the other nine commandments to remind the men of the fullness of the Law.

Finally, though, he stood up and said, "Let anyone among you who is without sin be the first to throw a stone at her." When the religious leaders heard it, they went away, one by one, beginning with the elders. Jesus was left alone with the woman standing before him. Rather than sharing in their judgment and even the legal requirements of the tradition he grew up in, he chose not to condemn the woman. Instead, simply, he told her not to do it again.

I want to suggest that a few things happened here, though the Bible is not explicit about it. Jesus felt everyone's feelings. Not only did he feel the judgmental anger of the men, but he also felt something deeper: their own shame. When you read this story, do you ever wonder why they brought the woman but not the man? Can a woman commit adultery all by herself? They reserved their judgment for the woman alone because they did not want to face their own sinfulness by seeing a man who was more like them than a woman. By bringing up their sinfulness, they all had to deal with their deeper feelings of shame and guilt.

One could suggest that Jesus reserved his empathy for the woman, and perhaps that is true. What we do know is that he withheld his judgment. Jesus cannot empathize with sin, but he can empathize with what it feels like to be accused and condemned. Condemnation and judgment shut down our ability to empathize. We judge others as a way of saying, "This person is not like me!" That is the opposite of empathy. Empathy says, "I am *like* this person."

We don't want to empathize with people we don't want to be like. Often something in that person reminds us of ourselves, and we don't want to admit it.

How can God possibly relate to us? God is without sin. If God looked at human beings with the idea that the main thing about them is that they are sinful, then God could experience no empathy, only judgment. But before there was sin in humanity, there was the image of God. God created humankind in God's own image. God sees God's own self in each person. God sees our goodness as well as our sin.

Remember the study from the Netherlands about religion and empathy. If a person views God as a God of judgment, it will lead them to judge others in the same way. But what if your God is one who loves people as they are, forgives their failures, and feels their feelings? If God is empathetic, can we learn to mirror God?

LETTING GO OF GROUP-ISH IDENTITY

The apostle Paul wrote in a letter to one of the churches he helped to start, "If one member suffers, all suffer together with it; if one member is honored, all rejoice together with it" (1 Cor 12:26). This is not a command or even advice. It is just a true statement. We suffer and rejoice with each other.

There is a qualifier, however: this is true if we share membership with the one who suffers or rejoices. We suffer and rejoice with people who are part of the same group, or clan, that we are.

For survival's sake, human beings began to form tribes. Tribes provide protection and provision. It is very hard to survive on your own. But imagine living in a world without Amazon, Walmart, or even a mom-and-pop corner market. Early humans faced wild animals, unfarmable land, horrible droughts, and hostile people who were also relying on the same food sources. We learned early on in our history as a species that it pays to be in a tribe. We need each other, especially when we are at our youngest and oldest stages of life. This clannish instinct is in our DNA. We learned to love our tribes and conform to their ways because to be rejected by the tribe was death. We like what the tribe likes, and we hate what the tribe hates. That same instinct lives in us today.

Jesus said it like this: "For if you love those who love you, what reward do you have? Do not even the tax collectors do the same? And if you greet only your brothers and sisters, what more are you doing than others? Do not even the Gentiles do the same?" (Matt 5:46–47).

It is not even particularly godly to love people who are *like* you. That is just a product of evolution. Jesus also said, "You have heard that it was said, 'You shall love your neighbor and hate your enemy.' But I say to you, Love your enemies and pray for those who persecute you" (Matt 5:43–44). To love like our God, we must love all people. It so goes against our group-ish instincts that it seems foolish, if not impossible, to love our enemies.

To love one's enemies begins with empathy. Subconsciously, we view all people who are different from us as a threat on some level. A team of Italian researchers conducted an experiment in which they had subjects watch videos of hands being pricked by a needle. They used hands of various skin colors. They also labeled the hands with different traits like religious affiliation. They observed brain images and muscle response in the subjects' hands to observe whether the participants responded as if their own hands were being pricked. The researchers found that the pain responses were reduced when the subject watched hands that were of a different color or a trait than their own. We naturally feel more empathy for people who are like us than for people who are different. It is our early human instincts in action.

Social work professor and author Elizabeth Segal teaches about a broader kind of empathy beyond our interpersonal relationship: social empathy. Segal defines social empathy as "the ability to understand people and other social groups by perceiving and experiencing their life situations. To do so involves learning about and understanding the historical context of group experiences, including the structural inequalities that have shaped communities." We can learn by listening to others. We would also benefit by becoming students of other cultures. The more we understand the communities that people grew up in, the more our empathy will increase for them.

Certainly we are very different from many people, but there is always a space to find commonality. To increase your empathy for people different from you, you might also find something you have in common. You might like the same sports team or have the same alma mater. Perhaps you both have young children or have been divorced. Maybe you both love Indian food. I believe a lot of empathy was created during the COVID-19 global pandemic. There is nothing like a harrowing shared experience to bring about empathy. And I cannot tell you how many conversations over the years I have had about people's experiences on 9/11. Every time I tell someone that I lived and worked in Manhattan on September 11, 2001, the person shares their experience, whether they were in Topeka or Rome. Tragedies that impact so many people end up creating common bonds. There are a million ways to establish an empathetic connection to another person. You just have to try.

That may be the problem for many people. They don't *want* to find out if they have anything in common with those of another political persuasion or worldview. Most people don't want to admit that they have anything in common with a serial murderer. Sometimes, when we cannot have empathy for someone, it is simply because we are afraid that we are more like them than we want to admit.

I remember when Osama bin Laden was killed by SEAL Team 6. That day was also something of a universal experience for Americans. A lot of people remember where they were. I was in a jazz club in New Orleans with my wife when the announcement began to spread like wildfire. Like many others, I had all kinds of feelings and emotions. I felt relief, sadness, tinges of old anger, and even some satisfaction that justice had been done.

A few weeks later, though, I read an interview with bin Laden's mother. She grieved her son's death, as well as the life that he had chosen to lead. Like a lightning bolt, it struck me that this villain had a mother who loved him too. Dare I admit that I had empathy for him? Could I believe that God loves bin Laden? We are both human beings who were once babies held by our mothers. Empathy entered my heart for her and even for him.

Christlike empathy is not limited to those who belong to our earthly clans and groups. When we see people as loved by the same God who loves us all unconditionally, we will find empathy rising in our hearts. We will then be able to share in the feelings of anyone and everybody if we so choose.

A WORD OF WARNING FOR THE HIGHLY EMPATHETIC

For those who are highly sensitive to others' feelings, empathy can be overwhelming. It is essential to distinguish between your feelings and experiences and the feelings and experiences of others. If you are a highly empathetic person who has not worked on self-differentiation, you are vulnerable to losing your sense of self. You may become a sponge, of sorts, for the suffering of others. Interestingly, if you are too empathetic and not self-differentiated, you may even open yourself to taking on the hatred and animosity and scorn that others are feeling.

No matter the specific emotion of another that you begin to feel as your own, in losing yourself in this way, you will not be able to be a helpful presence. If you are with anxious people, for instance, sharing their anxiety will just compound the anxiety. It is better to bring a non-anxious presence to anxious people and a non-angry presence to angry people. If you are un-self-differentiated, you will only inflame the problems and cause problems for yourself.

I know a hospital chaplain who was called into the emergency room where a boy had just died on the table. He entered the room and froze. The boy was the same age as his son. He was paralyzed, overwhelmed, and unable to be of help at all.

The chaplain's supervisor confronted him, gently but pointedly. He looked him in the eye and said softly, "That is not your son. I need you to say it: 'That is not my son.'" The chaplain needed this reminder to self-differentiate so that he would be able to do his job well. From then on, he tells me, whenever he walks into hospital rooms, he reminds himself, "That is not my son. That is not my daughter. That is not my wife. That is not my mother. That is not my dad. That is not me."

If we are unable to distinguish ourselves from others, it will lead to a condition called compassion fatigue. Ironically, you will become unable to care about other people because it has become simply exhausting. You will be emotionally numb to your own feelings as well.

Self-differentiation, combined with healthy empathy, combined with a healthy connection with God—that's spiritual intelligence. That combination will give you the ability to check people's emotional temperature without allowing their feelings to govern your own psyche. You can dip your toe into the feelings of another and see if it's hot or cold. That information will help you to best know how to respond to them with empathy but without jumping into the pool of their experience and drowning with them.

Feeling what others feel helps you to empathize with the experience of others, which in turn will help validate their experience. You will be able to be a mirror for them so they can see that their pain matters and that they are being loved through it.

CAN WE FEEL WHAT GOD IS FEELING?

An emotional bond forms with the people we grow attached to. The longer I have been married to my wife, the more we can sense each other's thoughts and feelings. She can tell when I am anxious. I can tell when she is worried. We can feel each other. We live in emotional resonance with each other but also with boundaries so we don't get entirely lost in worry or anxiety together.

The apostle Paul wrote, "For who has known the mind of the Lord so as to instruct him?" "But we have the mind of Christ" (1 Cor 2:16). It seems like an impossible thing that we might share in the mind of Christ, the one who Christians believe is God. Yet if it is true that God's Holy Spirit truly lives in human beings, and the Holy Spirit is also God, then God's thoughts and feelings can be discernible to us by looking within. Just as we can feel and sense the thoughts of people we have grown to know and love, then why couldn't this be the case in a relationship with God?

Our attachments inform and shape the way we feel and think. We become most like the things or people we love the most. Our minds were initially informed and shaped by the people who raised us. By shifting our attachment to God, we will allow our minds to be reshaped by God. Over time, as we grow in trust and love of God with regular communication and a sense that God is nearby, God will shape our feelings and thoughts.

It will always be important to distinguish between God within us and ourselves. We do not *become* God, any more than we become our parents or caregivers. But we can become like God, just as we become like our parents. We can feel God's love for people whom we would never love on our own. We can feel God's grief or God's anger over the troubled world. The more your attachment with God grows, the more your mind—your feelings and thoughts—will be informed and shaped by God.

It might seem like a far-out idea. I mean, could you be feeling God's feelings and thinking God's thoughts? Yes, if you love the Lord your God with all your heart, with all your soul, with all your mind, and with all your strength. Through your attachment to this loving God, God's love can flow through you to the world. People can experience the actual love of God through you. Loving others with God's love is what it means to have the mind of Christ.

REFLECTION QUESTIONS

1. When you see another person get hurt, how does it make you feel? Physically? Emotionally?

2. How have you experienced people's emotions? Sadness? Anger? Joy?

3. How were feelings expressed or not expressed in your family when you were growing up?

4. If you don't feel a lot of emotions, can you think of a time when you did? What changed?

5. Think of a time when another person showed that they understood how you were feeling. How did it feel to be understood?

SPIRITUAL INTELLIGENCE EXERCISE: MIRRORING FEELINGS

Most of us can feel what others are feeling if we learn to pay attention to others and ourselves.

When someone expresses anger, we often feel that anger inside of us. When someone smiles, we smile back without thinking. They are the same thing. As we discussed in this chapter, it's called mirroring, and it is the function of neurons called mirror neurons.

Over the next week, simply note how other people, whether in person or onscreen, alter your feelings. Recognize that those feelings are theirs, not yours. You are just mirroring them. This awareness will free you to be able to respond in the most loving way—both for them and for yourself.

PRAYER

Lord, I trust that you feel me. Let me feel your peace, compassion, and joy for me and others.

Dear God, I am afraid/angry/sad that _____.
Dear God, the world is afraid/angry/sad that_____.
Whatever feelings I have, I know that you feel them and validate them. I pray that in due time you will turn my fear into peace, anger into compassion, and sadness into joy. Amen.

9 | THE PATH OF RESPONDING TO OTHERS WITH LOVE

It was the lowest point of my life. A week earlier, I had come home from work to find a moving truck in front of our apartment building. My youthful marriage had been on the rocks. My spouse and I had both realized that our marriage wouldn't last, but she had taken the initiative I had been afraid to take. What I hadn't realized is that almost everything in the apartment was hers. All that was left was my cookery, my pillow, my clothes, and a green plastic lawn chair on the balcony.

When I looked at our bank balance, I found it just as empty as the apartment. Rent was overdue, and it would be another ten days until my next paycheck. The next day, there would be an eviction notice on my door unless I figured out a way to pay the rent. If ever I felt like the prodigal son, it was that day.

That day I said a prayer and went to work, desperate to figure out how to avoid eviction. Toward the end of the workday, when no solution had yet arisen, a face suddenly popped into my mind. John and I had started working for the company on the same day. I didn't know him well, but he seemed like a good guy.

I made my way over to his cubicle. John could tell something was wrong. I explained that I was desperate: I needed $650 for my rent by the next day, or else I would be evicted. He didn't ask for any explanation. He simply said, "Meet me at six o'clock at the coffee shop on the corner."

When I got to the coffee shop, I sat down in the booth, worried out of my mind. John walked in with a kind smile and sat across from me. He took an envelope out of his pocket and pushed it across the table. "There's enough money there to pay your rent and to get some groceries," he said. "Now tell me what's going on, Paul."

I began to explain that it might take me a long time to pay him back. "Paul, you are a good man, and I know you will pay me back," he said. "Now tell me what's going on." The compassion in his eyes opened something inside of me, and I began to share my story. He was the first person I had talked to about my failed marriage. I was so ashamed by everything that had transpired in the past year. He listened without judgment and assured me that he would be my friend through this. He urged me to talk to my parents as well.

I finally summoned the courage to tell my father, who helped me take control of my finances and begin to reestablish my credit. I began making a lot of changes in my life. Each paycheck, I would bring some money to John. Each time, I would apologize for how long it was taking me to pay him back. And each time, he would say the same thing, "Paul, you are a good man, and I know you will pay me back."

It would take me nearly a year to pay him back. When I handed John the final fifty dollars, he opened up his desk and pulled out an envelope. In it was every dollar I had paid him.

John held out the envelope to me. "It's here if you need it, okay? Just let me know."

I didn't know what to say, and I still don't. That is Christlike love—the kind of love that comes from God. It's the kind of love that Jesus meant when he said, "I give you a new commandment, that you love one another. Just as I have loved you, you also should love one another. By this everyone will know that you are my disciples, if you have love for one another" (John 13:35). The word for this kind of love in Greek is *agape*.

This word is read at many weddings from 1 Corinthians: "And now faith, hope, and love abide, these three; and the greatest of these is *love*." The traditional King James Version of the Bible translates *agape* as "charity": "But the greatest of these is charity." Today, *charity* has something of a negative connotation. Nobody wants to be a "charity case." But charity is indeed one of the ways to understand this kind of love. Charity means giving something to someone who is in need and expecting nothing in return.

God loves us charitably. We are indeed in need. Our parents loved us in our helpless neediness. Being cared for when we are helpless forms an attachment. While I have not seen John in years, he still holds a place in my heart. Every time someone in need asks me for help, I think of John and what he did for me— and not just *what* he did but *how* he did it, with such empathy.

God's agape love is not based on what we can give back; it is based on God's character as a loving God. It is like the love of a parent but is even more expansive. God's love is for all people. I have no doubt that if I had called my dad first instead of asking John for help, he would have done everything he could to help. I was just too ashamed to ask. My dad is also a very charitable man; if a stranger had asked him for help, he very well may have done the same. But many of us might be charitable toward our family members but not toward others. Agape love is like doing for a total stranger the same thing you would do for your own child.

A Hebrew word found in the Old Testament gives us an even deeper meaning: *hesed*. Psalm 136 is one of many examples of the use of *hesed* in referring to God: "O give thanks to the Lord, for he is good, for his *steadfast love* endures forever." Hesed is steadfast love. Not only does a parent help their child when they are in need; but in the best of circumstances, the love they show for their child is steadfast. God loves us without fail, not just sometimes. Agape is self-giving, and hesed is steady and unconditional. This kind of love is what all people need to grow in their ability to feel secure and ultimately to love people in the same way.

This path toward spiritual intelligence—of responding to others in love—is built on the previous eight paths. To act lovingly to others, we begin with our relationship with God— trusting, communicating, and recognizing God's nearness. Attaching our lives to God allows us to self-differentiate, which results in the ability to receive and give forgiveness, regulate our emotions, and be vulnerable in our relationships. Our relationship with God and our self-differentiation give us a greater capacity to empathize with others without being overwhelmed by their emotions.

Empathy allows us to listen, to feel what others feel, and to actively love our neighbors. It begins with God, and it leads to the very challenging act of loving others. Not just in theory or feeling but in real life. Not just when we feel like it but when love is needed.

THE LOVE THAT IS SHEER ACTION

Just before Jesus said, "Just as I have loved you, you also should love one another," he showed them what that love looks like. On the night before his death, Jesus got on his hands and knees and washed the feet of his disciples. Foot washing was reserved for servants and enslaved people, not rabbis and masters.

One time, one of my seminary professors asked the class, "Why is foot washing not a sacrament like baptism and the Lord's Supper are?" We as a class gave many astute answers, and the learned man shook his head to all of them. Finally, with gravitas and a slight grin, he said, "Because it's icky."

Loving others in the way of Jesus is dirty work sometimes, and it's icky. We are getting in between people's toes and scrubbing out the camel dung.

One of the most beautiful actions I ever saw in a church service happened during a Maundy Thursday communion and foot-washing service. I served a church that leased space to an apostolic Hispanic congregation, and we invited them to join us for this service. They showed us what foot washing was all about.

Many of the members of our congregation, which was primarily composed of white people, were reluctant to wash their feet or have their feet washed. The Hispanic worshippers jumped right in. Multiple people would wash each foot. As they washed, they prayed over the feet and even wept over them. When one elderly woman from my congregation went up front to have her feet washed, the Latinx believers must have washed her feet for fifteen minutes. They prayed and prayed and wept and wept. Their tears bathed her in love. Her tears flowed as well. Love flowed in a way I had never seen. They had never even met this woman, and yet they bathed her with their love.

The problem with our modern concept of charity is that there is a hierarchy of those who do the charity and those who receive it. Yes, it is serving, but it is hard to not think of yourself as better than the people you serve. But the way Jesus commands us to love others is reversed. The love of Jesus is one of deep humility, and it is icky. It is loving feet.

Søren Kierkegaard wrote, "Love is sheer action." Love may be supported by feelings and thoughts, but it is *always* an action. Love may be a feeling, but it is always a verb.

Jesus gives greater definition to this kind of love when he tells of the judgment day. In Matthew 25 appears this astonishing description of love. Look for the verbs.

When the Son of Man comes in his glory, and all the angels with him, then he will sit on the throne of his glory. All the nations will be gathered before him, and he will separate people one from another as a shepherd separates the sheep from the goats, and he will put the sheep at his right hand and the goats at the left. Then the king will say to those at his right hand, "Come, you that are blessed by my Father, inherit the kingdom prepared for you from the foundation of the world; for I was hungry and you gave me food, I was thirsty and you gave me something to drink, I was a stranger and you welcomed me, I was naked and you gave me clothing, I was sick and you took care of me, I was in prison and you visited me." Then the righteous will answer him, "Lord, when was it that we saw you hungry and gave you food, or thirsty and gave you something to drink? And when was it that we saw you a stranger and welcomed you, or naked and gave you clothing? And when was it that we saw you sick or in prison and visited you?" And the king will answer them, "Truly I tell you, just as you did it to one of the least of these who are members of my family, you did it to me." (Matt 25:31–36)

Love is very specific action based on the circumstances. Love is feeding a hungry person. Love is giving drink to a thirsty person. Love is welcoming a stranger. Love is providing clothes for those who need them. Love is taking care of a sick person. Love is visiting someone in prison. Love is encouraging someone who is discouraged. Love is listening to someone who needs to be heard. Love is helping someone pay their rent. Love is advocating for people nobody is listening to. Love is befriending a friendless person.

To wiggle around the import of this passage, you might try to figure out who is a member of Jesus's family and reserve your help for them. But the passage would suggest that you can assume that anyone you come across is Jesus himself.

In my second year of ministry at a small church in Nashville, my church decided to host a free dinner on Sunday nights. On the very first night, a man named Richard showed up. He had read about the dinner in the newspaper. He would not have called himself homeless because he lived in his truck and worked as a roofer. I would not have called him friendly. And if you had told me that fifteen years later, when I'd be living in another state, Richard would still be part of my life? Well, I would have laughed out loud.

It all started when I began helping Richard find work and occasionally buying him lunch. There was no shaking him. He'd mow my lawn and do odd jobs around the house. He'd show up at the church and help out with things for a few bucks. To be honest, I got a little weary of helping Richard. One December day when I was driving home from church, I asked God, "Why is Richard still in my life, and what the heck am I supposed to do about him?"

As I said this prayer, I noticed the song that was playing on the radio, "Grown-up Christmas List." It's a list of things that we might be asking for as mature, loving people: no more wars, no more harm, no more broken hearts. Just as I finished this prayer, these lyrics sang out to me: "Every man would have a friend." It brings tears to my eyes to this day. God did not put me in Richard's life for charity's sake. God put me here to be his friend.

I didn't realize how true this was until Richard was moving to Texas. A few years later, my family and I would happen to land in that state as well. To get there, Richard needed some gas for his journey. I met him at the station and filled up his tank. Before he got into his truck, he embraced me. "I love you," he said, and with tears in his eyes, he drove off.

Love may begin by helping someone in need, but it doesn't stop there. I think about the love of a parent. Parents help us when we are utterly incapable of helping ourselves, and it never ends.

THE LOVE OF A PARENT

One of the stories in the Bible that shows us what God's love is like is the parable of the prodigal son. You are probably familiar with the story, but it's so consequential and transformative that it's worth reading over and over again.

> Jesus said, "There was a man who had two sons. The younger of them said to his father, 'Father, give me the share of the property that will belong to me.' So he divided his property between them. A few days later the younger son gathered all he had and travelled to a distant country, and there he squandered his property in dissolute living. When he had spent everything, a severe famine took place throughout that country, and he began to be in need. So he went and hired himself out to one of the citizens of that country, who sent him to his fields to feed the pigs. He would gladly have filled himself with the pods that the pigs were eating, and no one gave him anything. But when he came to himself he said, 'How many of my father's hired

hands have bread enough and to spare, but here I am dying of hunger! I will get up and go to my father, and I will say to him, 'Father, I have sinned against heaven and before you; I am no longer worthy to be called your son; treat me like one of your hired hands.' So he set off and went to his father. But while he was still far off, his father saw him and was filled with compassion; he ran and put his arms around him and kissed him. Then the son said to him, 'Father, I have sinned against heaven and before you; I am no longer worthy to be called your son.' But the father said to his slaves, 'Quickly, bring out a robe—the best one—and put it on him; put a ring on his finger and sandals on his feet. And get the fatted calf and kill it, and let us eat and celebrate; for this son of mine was dead and is alive again; he was lost and is found!' And they began to celebrate." (Luke 15:11–24)

This young man really blew it. Not only did he ask for his inheritance before his father had even died; he then squandered it. When he returned to his father, he was so ashamed that he was planning on just asking to be one of his father's workers. By asking for his inheritance, he practically denied his father's existence; then, out of shame, he denied his place as his father's son. The father, though, embraced him and celebrated his return. The father's response is all love with no judgment.

That's not the end of the story. There is an older son, and he is not happy about his father's charity for his brother. Many of us more easily relate to him:

Now his elder son was in the field; and when he came and approached the house, he heard music and dancing. He called one of the slaves and asked what was going on. He replied, "Your brother has come, and your father has killed the fatted calf, because he has got him back safe and sound." Then he became angry and refused to go in. His father came out and began to plead with him. But he answered his father, "Listen! For all these years I have been working like a slave for you, and I have never disobeyed your command; yet you have never given me even a young goat so that I might celebrate with my friends. But when this son of yours came back, who has devoured your property with prostitutes, you killed the fatted calf for him!" Then the father said to him, "Son, you are always with me, and all that is mine is yours. But we had to celebrate and rejoice, because this brother of yours was dead and has come to life; he was lost and has been found." (Luke 15:25–32)

We cannot understand the depth of God's love until we have received what we do not deserve. God's love comes with grace. The father loved his older son the same as he loved the younger son, but the older son thought he deserved it more. He had everything, and nothing was lost for him. Perhaps the true difference between the brothers is that one of them knew he didn't deserve his father's love.

God loves all people no matter what. God loves all equally and without partiality. You might be thinking that you could never do that. If you are thinking about love as a feeling and something that must be returned, then you are right. God's love, though, is unconditional and never-ending. To be able to love others like God loves requires that we experience being loved like that.

Can you imagine if we loved everyone like the father in Jesus's parable loved? You can try to tell people how much God loves them, but the best way to spread that good news is loving others like Christ showed his disciples to love. That kind of love is what changes lives. Loving others like a truly loving parent loves a child is the most powerful way to spread the gospel.

LAVISHING LOVE

Before Jesus washed his disciples' feet, Mary of Bethany anointed his feet with a precious perfume worth three hundred denarii, which would be the equivalent of over fifty thousand dollars today. We will never know all the reasons Mary poured out such a precious amount of pure nard on Jesus's feet. Shortly before this event, Jesus brought her brother Lazarus back to life after being dead for over three days. How could she not love Jesus?

Mary's expression of love wasn't about help. It wasn't covering up any failure. It was a gift for the sake of giving. This kind of love is sacrificial. Mary gave what was perhaps her most valuable possession. It was costly, and it was personal. She needed a way to show her love. God's love is costly. Later that week, God's own son would give his life for the sake of showing God's love to the world. Just like this jar of precious essence, Jesus's life was broken and spilled.

God's love is freely given, but it will cost us to love others with that same love.

I met a thirteen-year-old girl and her brothers through a basketball ministry at the church I was with. Like many of the youths who came to us over the years in that basketball gym, Nesha did not have all the kinds of support and love that I had grown up with. Her mother did all a mother could do for her children, but she was working for two. Nesha's father was largely absent in her life, and when he was present, he was not helpful or loving.

One of the great joys of my ministry was baptizing Nesha, her brothers, and others who had become part of the church through the basketball ministry. Even as my wife and I moved on from Nashville to Dallas, I would still hear from many of the young people who are now adults, including Nesha. Nesha dreamed of being a nurse. She had completed two years of college but dropped out to help her family. She had a child of her own and another on the way. The father quickly disappeared. She was stuck, and she got evicted from her apartment.

I thought of John, the man who had helped me all those years ago. I thought of my parents. I heard God whispering to me, "She is your daughter. Do for her as your parents have done for you. Do for her as you would your own daughter." I drove to Tennessee and loaded up Nesha's stuff and her child and drove her to our home, where she could figure out what her next steps were.

As she was getting closer to having her second child, she decided to move back to be near her mother. She had found another apartment and a job. She had her second child. Life was a struggle. She worked hard and was able to pay her bills, but her dream of becoming a nurse was fading away. God whispered to me, "Paul, she is your daughter. Do for her as your parents have done for you. Do for her as you would your own daughter." My parents paid for my college. I worked and paid for my car. I had some scholarships that took care of my housing. I had a lot of help. Yes, she could get grants that would pay for her tuition. She also could get aid from the state to cover her childcare. But it was not possible for her to go to school and meet all her expenses without going into major debt. My wife and I decided that we would help her until she finished the nursing program.

Nesha went to school during the week, from seven to four, and worked in the evenings and on the weekends. She studied as hard as any person I have ever known, and with little sleep while raising children. I could write a whole book about the trials she faced in these two years. Nesha persevered. God made the way, but she walked it. One of the most joyful moments of my life was when my whole family traveled to Nashville to watch her graduate. Nesha is a different person. She is reborn.

I had held back this kind of hesed love in the past because I thought, *If I can't do it for everyone, then I can't do it for this person.* I thought that agape love would cost me too much. But God doesn't call us to do this for everyone. I believe God brings certain people in our lives for us to love as our own. Some we give birth to. Some we adopt. Some we baptize. Some drift into our lives for a day or even a season. Some remain with us for years. As far as the cost is concerned, remember that God is taking care of you. None of us is on our own, burdened with our own survival. God brings people and sources of provision into our lives as well. The way of responding to others with love is in part the way God takes care of the world.

When Mary of Bethany poured out her precious gift of pure nard on Jesus's feet, the fragrance filled the room. For some in the room, it was too much. What a waste, some said. Perhaps they were uncomfortable seeing this woman on her knees using her hair to wipe the excess from his feet. But I imagine others were moved to the depths of their souls. Perhaps they intuited Mary's deep spiritual intelligence, even if they didn't know what to call it.

I believe Jesus recognized her lovingness, the spiritually intelligent way Mary approached the world. He said, "Leave her alone. She bought it so that she might keep it for the day of my burial. You always have the poor with you, but you do not always have me" (John 12:7). Jesus knew that he would soon die on a cross, loving the world. Perhaps Mary understood this as well.

Anointing someone else's feet is likely an icky thing, yet it is perhaps a more vulnerable position to bare your feet to another and be loved in your ickiness. Jesus showed us this as well. He let Mary love him. Perhaps he even needed it during that week in which he would be falsely accused, condemned, and executed.

Is it a coincidence that shortly after having his own feet anointed, Jesus washed the feet of his beloved disciples? Spiritually intelligent people call forth the spiritual intelligence of others. Lovingness calls for and inspires more lovingness. Perhaps Christ would even be inspired by your love of others. I am sure that God loves when we show love to others. And those around us need it desperately.

The love of God working through your life—spiritual intelligence—is like the fragrance of costly perfume. When we love in the way of Christ, our love can quietly and gently transform our homes, our churches, our workplaces, our neighborhoods, and every unloved person who God leads into our lives.

Many people are praying to be loved even if they don't know it. They are crying out like unloved babies needing care. We can follow the path of responding to others with love.

REFLECTION QUESTIONS

1. What would you think or feel if you had been in the room when Mary anointed Jesus's feet?

2. When has someone lavished love on you?

3. What ways might you love and serve others more sacrificially?

4. Is there anyone who you feel that you could not love in the manner of how Jesus or Mary loved others? Why?

SPIRITUAL INTELLIGENCE EXERCISE: EXTRAVAGANT LOVE

Give or do something extravagant for a person God has brought into your life. Do it with love.

PRAYER

O Lord, you are love. Everything you say or do is out of love and is the definition of love. Remove anything in me that keeps me from receiving your love for me and lavishing that love on others.

Dear God, remove my _____ so that I may experience and share your love.

Lead me to the actions I need to take to let go of anything that keeps me from your love. Amen.

EPILOGUE

When I first took an emotional intelligence assessment during my doctoral studies, I was dismayed that my scores were average. The instructor gave us a piece of good news, though. Unlike IQ, emotional intelligence can be developed and increased. The corporate world was beginning to embrace emotional intelligence, and the concept was really aiding in employee enrichment and leadership development.

We need greater emotional intelligence in our leaders. Change in the leaders means change in organizations and churches over time. Yet the church is slow to embrace secular concepts of human development. Plus, how can Christians develop emotional intelligence without considering how their relationship with God fits in?

Hence, I began to pursue a model of spiritual intelligence that is grounded in a relationship with God and includes relationship with ourselves and others. What good is a relationship with God if it does not change the way we relate to others and ourselves?

I began developing a theory of spiritual intelligence and an assessment to aid the church and individuals pursuing spiritual and emotional development in their journey.

In the pages of this book, you have read the fullest expression of my theory. So what comes next? You might now consider taking the assessment that measures how you are currently faring on each of the nine paths you are walking.

The assessment, which I mentioned in the introduction, is called the GPS Spiritual Inventory. You can take the GPS at www.soul-metrics.com. You will receive a sixteen-page report to aid you on your journey of loving God, self, and neighbor. If you wish to speak to a coach, counselor, or spiritual director to guide you in taking your next steps in spiritual development, you can reach out to us on the same website.

The GPS measures the same nine areas you just learned about in this book:

ATTACHMENT TO GOD

1. Trusting
2. Communicating
3. Nearness

SELF-DIFFERENTIATION

1. Forgiveness
2. Emotional regulation
3. Vulnerability

EMPATHY

1. Listening
2. Feelings
3. Loving

I have personally worked with hundreds of people on these nine aspects of spiritual intelligence and seen amazing progress. I have experienced progress in my own life—although I have a long way to go in every category, from trust in God to forgiveness to empathy.

The spiritual journey is not a solo journey. God calls us into community. Consider forming a group at your church or in your neighborhood to work through this book. We need partners to hear us and to encourage us along the way.

The spiritual journey is also not an easy one. Much of our spiritual development comes from facing our fears, our shames, and our wounds and inviting God into every part of who we are. The results are worth the effort.

God sees us as we are, and we see God's loving face directed at us. Through this loving gaze, we begin a transformation into the image of God we see in Christ. It doesn't happen magically overnight, but by degrees, in time, and through your relationship with God, you will become more like the God who made you than the world that raised you. You will become your most loving self, the person God always hoped you would be.

I began this journey for myself and the people God entrusted to my care. Those who rely on me and interact with me—my children, my wife, and the churches and individuals I serve—feed off my own spiritual life. I cannot just teach concepts to people; it is through loving relationships that people develop and grow. Nothing gives me greater joy than to see my own children learning to have empathy and show love for others.

As I wrote this epilogue, I received a text from Nesha, who is about to begin her career as a nurse. She just wanted to say she was grateful for the support my wife and I had given her. She wrote, "I couldn't have made it this far without you all." I responded, "None of us makes it alone." And then the most wonderful response came back: "I've been thinking about this. I wanted to see if there is a place where a speaker could go to tell their hardship stories that led to success. To talk to a group of individuals around my age group or even teenagers." This is how it works: loving others leads to loving others.

You have greater power than you know to change people's lives. All it takes is receiving the love that God has brought into your life and the will to share it with others. Love begets love begets love begets love.

ACKNOWLEDGMENTS

God's support, encouragement, and love have come to me through some amazing human beings. It took a village to raise this book! I want to thank:

My wife, Jennifer, for believing in me and doing the lion's share of bringing home the bacon while I pursued my dream of bringing spiritual intelligence into the practice of ministry and in written form through this book;

My mom, Judy Burns, for showing me unconditional and sacrificial love my whole life;

My dad, Jim Burns, for not only encouraging me to write this book but also walking with me to the finish line;

My brothers, David and John, who have been my constant cheerleaders as I sought to bring something new into the world;

My therapist, who continues to invite me into self-care and who believed in my cause of bringing spiritual intelligence into the world;

Austin Presbyterian Theological Seminary (Austin, Texas) for molding my faith into theological and practical terms;

Priest Lake Presbyterian Church in Nashville for allowing a young pastor with radical ideas to experiment with ministry and for loving me along the way;

First Presbyterian Church of Garland, Texas, for their support as I worked through the arduous task of completing my doctor of ministry degree and their blessing as I left pastoral work to pursue the practical research that led to this book;

St. Mark Presbyterian Church of Dallas, Texas, for allowing me to preach through these concepts on the way to writing this book;

United Presbyterian Church of Greenville, Texas, for giving me the opportunity to practice ministry and giving me very needed employment while I wrote this book;

Western Seminary in Portland, Oregon, for challenging me to pursue innovative ministry ideas for the sake of the kingdom of God;

Dr. Chad Hall, who led and designed the program that introduced me to many of the subjects, like emotional intelligence and neuropsychology, that went into the stew pot that became spiritual intelligence;

Dr. Kenneth Logan, my dissertation adviser, who continues to be an instrumental partner in my research and thinking;

My editor and the whole team at Broadleaf Books for saying yes to my project and for making it all that it needed to be;

Gretchen Martens, my writing coach, for her encouragement and facilitation of the writing process, especially when I was stuck like a stick-in-the-mud;

Dr. Sim Hassler, who has been my ministry coach for over fourteen years and who helps me to know that who I am as a child of God far outweighs anything I do;

My constant companion, the Holy Spirit, who leads me with grace and love always and who taught me to trust God in ways I never thought possible;

Jesus, who continues to teach me and show me what love is;

And last but not least, my ever-loving fatherly, motherly God, my Abba, who welcomes me with open arms and fatted calves whenever I acknowledge God's presence in my life.

NOTES

INTRODUCTION

George Barna identified ten stops: George Barna, *Maximum Faith: Live Like Jesus* (New York: Metaformation, 2011).

In fact, emotional intelligence has proven: Travis Bradberry and Jean Greaves. *Emotional Intelligence 2.0* (San Diego, CA: TalentSmart, 2009), 21.

Attachment theory pioneer John Bowlby described a person: John Bowlby, *Attachment*, vol. 1 of Attachment and Loss Series (New York: Basic Books, 1982).

The singer sang of God's presence and power: The Lord Thy God by Blaine Morris 1986 performed by the Brooklyn Taber-nacle Choir.

CHAPTER 1

When someone listens to you: Curt Thompson, *Anatomy of the Soul: Surprising Connections between Neuroscience and Spiritual Practices That Can Transform Your Life and Relationship* (Carrolton, TX: Tyndale Momentum, 2010), 137.

CHAPTER 2

My favorite saint, Mister Rogers, said: Fred Rogers, *The World According to Mister Rogers* (Westport, CT: Hyperion, 2003), 59.

In the 1960s, psychologist Mary Ainsworth designed: For more on this experiment, see Saul Mcleod, "Mary Ainsworth: Strange Situation Experiment and Attachment Theory," Simply Psychology, updated August 5, 2023, https://www.simplypsychology.org /mary-ainsworth.html.

CHAPTER 3

John Bowlby, the pioneer of attachment theory, wrote: Pehr Granqvistand and Lee. A. Kirkpatrick, *Attachment and Religious Representations and Behavior. Handbook of Attachment*, 3rd ed. (New York: Guilford Press, 2018), 921.

Then I read these words of Lewis's: C. S. Lewis, *Mere Christianity* (San Francisco: Harper, 2001), 168.

CHAPTER 4

Biblical scholar William Barclay writes: William Barclay, *The Letters to the Galatians and Ephesians (The New Daily Study Bible)* (Louisville, KY: Westminster John Knox Press, 2002), 156.

Conversely, forgiveness can actually calm our stress: "Forgiveness: Your Health Depends on It," Johns Hopkins Medicine, accessed August 29, 2023, https://www.hopkinsmedicine .org/health/wellness-and-prevention/forgiveness-your-health -depends-on-it#:~:text=Chronic%20anger%20puts%20you %20into,levels%2C%20leading%20to%20improved%20 health.

Robert Quinn, an expert on organizational leadership: Robert Quinn, *Deep Change: Discovering the Leader Within* (Hoboken, NJ: Jossey-Bass, 1996).

In her book **The Body Is Not an Apology:** Sonya Renee Taylor, *The Body Is Not an Apology: The Power of Radical Self-Love* (Oakland, CA: Berrett-Koehler, 2018), 4.

CHAPTER 5

In a sense, humans have not one brain but three: "The Triune Brain," The Science of Psychotherapy, October 26, 2016, https://www.thescienceofpsychotherapy.com/the-triune-brain/.

But a resonance develops between child and caretaker: Thomas Lewis, Fari Amini, and Richard Lannon, *A General Theory of Love* (New York: Vintage Anchor Publishing, 2000).

Their answer: "No. These things leave you more vulnerable": Emily Nagoski and Amelia Nagoski, *Burnout: The Secret to Unlocking the Stress Cycle* (New York: Ballantine Books, 2019), 156.

CHAPTER 6

"Shame is the intensely painful feeling": Brené Brown, *Daring Greatly: How the Courage to Be Vulnerable Transforms the Way We Live, Love, Parent, and Lead* (New York: Penquin Random House, 2012), 69.

He continues, "This is no easy task": Curt Thompson, *The Soul of Shame: Retelling the Stories We Believe about Ourselves* (Downers Grove, IL: InterVarsity Press, 2015), 104–105.

Henri Nouwen, in* The Wounded Healer, *writes: Henri Nouwen, *The Wounded Healer* (London: Darton, Longman, and Todd, 1994).

CHAPTER 7

Children's television icon Fred Rogers: Fred Rogers, *You Are Special: Words of Wisdom for All Ages from a Beloved Neighbor* (New York: Penguin, 1995).

"Find someone to listen to you": John Fox, "When Someone Deeply Listens to You," in *Spiritual Literacy: Reading the Sacred in Everyday Life*, ed. Mary Ann Brussat and Frederic Brussat (New York: Touchstone, 1998), 454.

A 2013 study from the Max Planck Institute: Laila van Ments, Peter Roelofsma, and Jan Treur, "Modelling the Effect of Religion on Human Empathy Based on An Adaptive Temporal–Causal Network Model," *Computational Social Networks* 5, no. 1 (2018): 1, https://www.ncbi.nlm.nih.gov/pmc/articles/PMC5756277/.

This projection of our feelings is referred to: "I'm Ok, You're Not Ok," The Max Plank Society, October 9, 2013, https://www.mpg.de/research/supramarginal-gyrus-empathy.

A University of Toronto study on empathy: Tina Adamopoulos, "U of T Researchers Explore the Concept of Empathy in Everyday Life," July 26, 2021, https://www.utoronto.ca/news/u-t-researchers-explore-concept-empathy-everyday-life#:~:text=The%20researchers%20found%20that%20people%20will%20empathize%20when,emotions%20without%20flagging%20them%20as%20opportunities%20to%20empathize.

Psychiatrist Curt Thompson writes: Thompson, *Anatomy of the Soul*, 137.

CHAPTER 8

In 1990, researchers in Italy were observing the brain: Maddalena Fabbri-Destro and Giacomo Rizzolatti, "Mirror Neurons and Mirror Systems in Monkeys and Humans," *Physiology* 23, no. 3 (2008): 171–179, https://journals.physiology.org/doi/full/10.1152/physiol.00004.2008.

A 2018 study out of the Netherlands: Laila van Ments, Peter Roelofsma, and Jan Treur, "Modelling the Effect of Religion on Human Empathy Based on an Adaptive Temporal-Causal Network Model," *Computational Social Networks* 5, no. 1 (January 5, 2018), https://www.ncbi.nlm.nih.gov/pmc/articles/PMC5756277/.

A team of Italian researchers conducted an experiment: Alessio Avenanti et al., "Stimulus-Driven Modulation of Motor-Evoked Potentials during Observation of Others' Pain," *NeuroImage* 32 (2006): 316–324, http://www.alessioavenanti.com/pdf_library/avenanti_2006neuroimage.pdf.

Segal defines social empathy as: Elizabeth A. Segal, *Social Empathy: The Art of Understanding Others* (New York: Columbia University Press, 2018), 4.

CHAPTER 9

Søren Kierkegaard wrote: Søren Kierkegaard, *Works of Love* (New York: Harper Perennial Modern Thought, 2009), 68.